"*Good News to the Poor* is good news for readers thinking through the relationship of evangelism to social action. Tim Chester rightly emphasizes the centrality of the gospel as he compares dependency-creating welfare with dignity-embracing development."

Marvin Olasky, Editor in Chief, World News Group

"The Christian church has at its best been known for its exemplary love and sacrificial service to 'the least of these': the poor, the oppressed, and the marginalized. Tim Chester shows that gospel proclamation and tangible acts of love, service, and mercy toward our neighbors should not be pitted against each other—God's grace motivates action, and words and deeds go together."

Justin Holcomb, Director of Resurgence; Pastor, Mars Hill Church, Seattle, Washington

"Tim Chester provides a timely reminder that Christianity at its best is actually a well-balanced combination of social action and gospel proclamation. This book does an excellent job removing the perceived wall between these two camps. Chester challenges the Christian church to work for justice and peace in the process of calling individuals to conversion. This book is a much-needed call for a renewed understanding of the Christian calling."

Ben Peays, Executive Director, The Gospel Coalition

"What's the relationship between the gospel and social action for the believer? I've been asked that question many times over the years, and it is one we must answer well. If we do not get the relationship between the gospel and social action right, we will likely end up undermining both of them. This is why Tim Chester's *Good News to the Poor* is an essential book for Christians. He argues persuasively and winsomely that gospel proclamation and social action are inseparable."

Dan Cruver, Director, Together for Adoption; author, *Reclaiming Adoption: Missional Living through the Rediscovery of Abba Father*

"This important, well-written book is a must-read for those looking for a way to integrate word-and-deed to advance God's purposes in our needy world."

Tom Sine, author, *Living on Purpose: Finding God's Best for Your Life*

"A vital challenge to gospel people to follow in the footsteps of William Carey. Consistent, mission-minded evangelicals have always refused to choose between a commitment to gospel proclamation and an active concern for the poor. Tim Chester digs deep into the Bible to show us why both are vital and what it means to be Christ's people in a world of need."

Keith Walker, Director, Serving in Mission, UK/Northern Europe

GOOD
NEWS
TO THE
POOR

Other Crossway books by Tim Chester:

Everyday Church: Gospel Communities on Mission (with Steve Timmis), 2012

A Meal with Jesus: Discovering Grace, Community, and Mission around the Table, 2011

You Can Change: God's Transforming Power for Our Sinful Behavior and Negative Emotions, 2010

Total Church: A Radical Reshaping around Gospel and Community (with Steve Timmis), 2008

GOOD
NEWS
TO THE
POOR

SOCIAL INVOLVEMENT
AND THE GOSPEL

TIM CHESTER

CROSSWAY

WHEATON, ILLINOIS

Library of Congress Cataloging-in-Publication Data

Chester, Tim.
  Good news to the poor : social involvement and the gospel / Tim Chester.
     pages   cm
  Originally published: Nottingham, England : Inter-Varsity Press, c2004.
  Includes bibliographical references and index.
  ISBN 978-1-4335-3703-5
  1. Church work with the poor. 2. Evangelistic work.
3. Missions. 4. Social gospel. 5. Church group work. I. Title.
BV639.P6C44   2013
261.8—dc23   2013002367

Contents

Acknowledgments

This book began life as a series of seminars at Spring Harvest Word Alive 2002. Thanks belong to John Risbridger of UCCF (Universities and Colleges Christian Fellowship) and Hugh Palmer of Word Alive for encouraging me to return to these issues, and to Keith Walker of UCCF and SIM (Serving In Mission) whose idea it was to turn them into a book. In June 2003 I presented much of the material in the book at the Kampala Evangelical School of Theology (KEST), Uganda. The opportunity to reflect on the issues with the staff and students of KEST was a great privilege. I want to express my thanks to them for their invitation and for the warm welcome I and my daughter, Katie, received during our time in Uganda. I also presented some of this material at a Micah Network consultation in Sarajevo, Bosnia, in November 2003. Once again, the opportunity to discuss these issues with churches and organizations working in the Balkans and Central Asia was an enriching experience.

Dewi Hughes, Daniel Strange, Keith Walker, Julian Hardyman, and Stephanie Heald all made encouraging and critical comments on drafts. Sarah Hill of Tearfund tracked down references and information for me with her typical verve. The book is dedicated to Dewi, a friend and former colleague, whose teaching and example have often encouraged and challenged me.

Tim Chester
Sheffield

Introduction

Let me introduce Albert. Albert calls himself a postevangelical. He says there are many good things about the evangelical church in which he grew up, but he himself has grown out of evangelicalism's narrowness. Like his postmodern friends, he is wary of truth claims, and instead he wants to emphasize symbols and images. This makes him much more comfortable with social involvement than with evangelism. Evangelism makes him uneasy because, as he puts it, "we are all on a faith journey" and he thinks that evangelism among the poor is simply manipulative. His catchphrase is "don't force your truth on others." Instead we should walk with the poor, care for them, and help them on their faith journey while expecting them to enrich our own faith journeys.

Then there is Brian. Brian happily calls himself a conservative evangelical. As far as he is concerned, the main task of the church is preaching the gospel. He is regularly involved in open-air preaching and door-to-door visitation. He sees any form of social involvement as a return to the social gospel, a movement at the beginning of the twentieth century that believed the kingdom of God could come in history through Christian social action. He complains about trendy new Christian organizations doing social work and diverting money from traditional missionary agencies. As far as he is concerned, and he is not slow to tell you this, "social action is heresy." In fact, however, he has taken action on abortion because he sees these as undermining the Christian foundations of the nation.

Meet Catherine. Catherine is unashamedly an evangelical. She believes strongly in the authority of the Bible and is enthusiastic about evangelism—she is heavily involved in the seekers' course in her church. But when people say that the church should focus on preaching, her hackles rise. She points out that the Bible has a lot to say about the poor and the need to care for both physical and spiritual needs. She thinks it is unhelpful to say that one thing is more important than another. "Physical and spiritual together" is her motto. She has spent many hours arguing it out with people like Brian in her church. Every time the church discusses reaching its community or spending its missionary funds, the argument starts up again.

Finally, let me introduce Douglas. Douglas is the minister of an evangelical church that is popular with students from the nearby university. He is committed to an expository ministry because he believes the Word is central to Christian mission and Christian experience. Douglas sees students affected by the relativism of their peers and the postmodernism of their lecturers. He sees them lacking the confidence to share the gospel with their friends and opting for social involvement as a socially acceptable alternative. He fears that people like Albert are leading evangelicals back into liberalism. He acknowledges the validity of Christian social involvement, and he is happy for his church to have Social Action Sunday each year devoted to the needs of the world's poor. But he wants to reassert the centrality of the Word and the priority of Word-centered ministry.

All these examples are based on real people. But, as they say, their names have been changed to protect their identities. Their positions characterize—and perhaps caricature—the ongoing debate about social involvement and its place in mission. Is social involvement something we do as well as evangelism? Is it another way of doing evangelism? Or perhaps it is a distraction from the real job of proclaiming the gospel? This book explores these issues. My aim is to look at the issue of social involvement and our responsibility to the poor in the light of the nature, content, and priorities of the gospel. I hope this gospel focus might move us beyond another restatement of the case of social involvement or another look at how social involvement and evangelism fit together.

I have introduced the four characters above not only to present the issues but also to make an important preliminary observation. Catherine has always discussed these issues with people like Brian. She has spent her life trying to persuade the Brians of this world that social involvement is legitimate. Douglas, on the other hand, has people like Albert in mind when he thinks about these issues. He has real concerns about the effect that Albert's ideas are having on young Christians. When Catherine and Douglas come together, they appear poles apart. When they talk to each other, Catherine thinks she is still arguing with Brian, and Douglas thinks he is arguing with Albert. The debate gets heated, and there appears to be no agreement. But I want to suggest that Catherine and Douglas may be much closer to each other than they realize. Chapters 1 and 2 look at the strength of Catherine's position, while chapter 3 looks at the strength of Douglas's position. Chapter 4 explores how their positions might fit together.

Sometimes people draw distinctions between social concern, social involvement, socio-political action, community development, and so on. Certainly there are different forms of social involvement. They range from simply providing a person's immediate needs to challenging the economic and political structures of a society. These distinctions are significant, but I do not want to load too much weight onto particular words. I will use the various terms in a fairly fluid and interchangeable way, making distinctions explicit only when they are significant. By social involvement, I mean both a concern for those within the Christian community and the Christian community caring for the needs of its neighbors in the wider society and offering a place of belonging. It can also include changing the policies, structures, and culture of society through social reform. But social reform will always be limited prior to the return of Christ. Above all, the church witnesses to the coming reign of God. Although many of the arguments in this book apply to wider social issues as well as involvement in the arts and culture, I have focused on issues of poverty. I see poverty, however, not simply as economic deprivation but in terms of social marginalization and powerlessness.

The book aims to present a biblical case for evangelical social action. But I also want to offer a critique of some of the theology and practice of social action within evangelicalism. I will criticize the arguments of some proponents of Christian social action. This does not mean I am opposed to social action itself. Rather I want to construct an approach to social action that is shaped by the gospel—a genuinely *evangelical* social action in the truest meaning of the word *evangelical*. Howard Peskett and Vinoth Ramachandra say, "It [has] often (sadly) been the case that evangelicals who are outspoken campaigners against social evils tend to be marginalized by conservative churches, and so inevitably drift towards the more "radical" end of the theological spectrum."[1] I want to urge conservatives not to marginalize those who uphold the cause of the oppressed and to urge social activists not to go down the blind alley of theological liberalism.

---

[1] Howard Peskett and Vinoth Ramachandra, *The Message of Mission* (Nottingham, UK: Inter-Varsity, 2003), 255.

1

The Case for Social Involvement

I stood in Sector 12 among small, squat houses roofed with plastic weighted down with rubbish. With me was Dr. Kiran Martin, director of ASHA, a Christian organization working in the slums of Delhi. Around us a crowd gathered, eager to talk. Most of the men had jobs—railway workers, construction site laborers, balloon sellers. Some of the one-room houses had a television, the electricity tapped off from the mains. There was a communal toilet block, above which ASHA has a small clinic. When we asked if anyone ever escaped the slum, the answer was no. The only jobs available are low paid with long hours. Most people cannot even read bus numbers. Alcoholism and crime are common. People are subject to slum landlords—protectors and oppressors at one and the same time. Standing there, I realized that the problem for these people was not simply lack of material possessions but powerlessness.

When Kiran Martin graduated as a doctor, she had the opportunity for a well-paid job and a comfortable life. Instead, starting with just a table and chair, she has given herself in the service of the poor. Several years on, ASHA impacts the lives of 150,000 slum dwellers, empowering communities by training health workers and lobbying government to improve slum conditions. Kiran Martin has invested time in building relationships with slum landlords, hosting an annual meal for them. She persuaded them to see that it was in everybody's interest to tackle some of the problems that were oppressing the slum dwellers. In the same way, she has built relationships with local government officials so that they have been willing to trust resources to ASHA. Through patience and allowing officials to share the credit for achievements, ASHA has also been able to negotiate government-funded slum redevelopments. Now the government's new housing policy has adopted the model used by ASHA to transform slums into established communities.

But that is not all: in Sector 12 there is now a church of twenty-five converts from Hinduism. This is an area known for its Hindu extremism. But everywhere Kiran Martin walks in the slums, she is greeted warmly. Church planting that had proved impossible in the past was now possible because of the trust and respect built by Kiran Martin in Christ's name.

The Example of William Carey

I visited Kiran Martin's work in Delhi in 1993. Two hundred years before, in 1793, William Carey arrived in India. Ruth and Vishal Mangalwadi begin their appreciation of Carey with a fictional quiz. They imagine a competition for Indian university students in which the question is asked: "Who was William Carey?" The first reply is that William Carey was a botanist who published the first books on the natural history of India, who introduced new systems of gardening, and after whom a variety of eucalyptus was named. Next, an engineering student says William Carey introduced the steam engine to India and began the first indigenous paper and printing industries. Another student sees Carey as a social reformer who successfully campaigned for women's rights; another as a campaigner for the humane treatment of lepers. An economics student points out that Carey introduced savings banks to combat usury. Carey is credited with starting the first newspaper in any oriental language. He conducted a systematic survey of Indian agricultural practices and founded the Indian Agri-Horticultural Society, thirty years before the Royal Agricultural Society was established in England. Carey was the first to translate and publish the religious classics of India and wrote the first Sanskrit dictionary for scholars. He founded dozen of schools, providing education for people of all castes, boys and girls. He pioneered lending libraries and wrote the first essays on forestry in India. To a significant degree he transformed the ethos of the British administration in India from colonial exploitation to a genuine sense of civil *service*.

And so it goes on with Carey's contribution to science, engineering, industry, economics, medicine, agriculture and forestry, literature, education, social reform, public administration, and philosophy all being celebrated.[1] Yet most of us know William Carey as the cobbler from England who became a pioneer missionary and evangelist. Who was the real William Carey? The answer is that Carey was all these things and more.

The Example of Early Christians

Christians have a long history of being involved in social issues—care for the poor; involvement in the arts, science, and culture; participation in civil society; campaigning in the political arena. Tertullian, the North African theologian, writing at the end of the second century after Christ, famously described how his fellow Christians shared with each other:

> If he likes, each puts in a small donation; but only if it he wants to and only if he is able. There is no compulsion; all is voluntary. These gifts are, as it were, piety's deposit fund. For they are not taken and spent on feasting and drinking-sessions, but to support and bury poor people, to supply the wants of needy boys and girls without parents, and of house-bound old people. . . . People say, See how they love one another. . . . One in mind and soul, we do not hesitate to share our earthly goods with one another. We have all things in common except our wives.[2]

---

[1] Ruth and Vishal Mangalwadi, *Carey, Christ and Cultural Transformation: The Life and Influence of William Carey* (Carlisle, UK: OM, 1993), 1–8.
[2] Tertullian, *Apology*, 39.

Writing in a similar vein at about the same time, Irenaeus said:

> Instead of tithes which the law commanded, the Lord said to divide everything we have with the poor. . . . Those who have received freedom set aside all their possessions for the Lord's purposes, giving joyfully and freely and not just the least valuable of their possessions.[3]

Basil the Great, writing in the fourth century AD, warned his readers:

> The bread which you keep, belongs to the hungry; the coat which you preserve in your wardrobe, to the shoeless; the gold which you have hidden in the ground, to the needy. Wherefore, as often as you were able to help others, and refused, so often did you do them wrong.[4]

During this period the church was seeing significant and widespread growth. About half a million new members were added every generation. By the beginning of the fourth century the numbers had risen to five million—about 8 percent of the Roman Empire—despite periodic persecution and constant revilement. These twin factors of gospel growth and persecution led to the first apologetics. These were not only appeals for toleration but also for conversion. One of the most prominent early apologists was Justin Martyr. Justin was from a pagan background, but, being born in Samaria, he probably would have been familiar with Judaism. He spent some time wandering around the Mediterranean looking for a worldview that made sense to him. He was finally converted through a chance encounter with an old man on the shore near Ephesus. After his conversion he became an evangelist and, although traveling widely, spent most of his life in Rome, where he was martyred in AD 163.

Justin wrote an *Apology* addressed to the emperor some time

---

[3] Irenaeus, *Against Heresies*, 4.13.3.
[4] Cited in Duncan B. Forrester, *On Human Worth: A Christian Vindication of Equality* (London: SCM, 2001), 114.

after AD 151 in which he attempted carefully to explain Christianity in a context where it was being misunderstood. Typically the apologists like Justin who wrote to a Roman audience focused on the civil consequences of Christianity. Describing the supposedly secret gatherings of Christians, Justin says: "They who are well to do, and willing, give what each thinks fit; and what is collected is deposited with the president, who succours the orphans and widows and those who, through sickness or any other cause, are in want, and those who are in bonds and the strangers sojourning among us, and in a word takes care of all who are in need."[5]

Justin recognizes that in one sense Christianity *is* subversive. It operates with a set of values that is contrary to elements of Roman society and culture. So he is not afraid to argue for the moral superiority of Christianity. The concern of the early church was not confined to other Christians. The Christians, for example, would collect unwanted children, left on the city rubbish dumps to die, and rear them themselves. Justin says: "But as for us, we have been taught that to expose newly-born children is the act of wicked men; and this we have been taught so that we should not do anyone an injury and so that we should not sin against God."[6] Justin describes how many of the children exposed were taken to be brought up as prostitutes, and this he strongly condemns. He says to the emperor: "You even collect pay and levies and taxes from these [prostitutes] whom you ought to exterminate from your civilized world. . . . You charge against us the actions that you commit openly and treat with honour."[7] Justin does not hesitate to condemn social injustice and call on the emperor to change his policies. What is striking about this is that it comes in the context of a plea for tolerance toward Christians.

Nevertheless, although elements of Christianity run contrary to the values of Roman society, Justin wants to show that Christianity is good for society. "We are in fact of all men your best

---

[5] Justin, *Apology*, 1.67.
[6] Ibid., 1.27.
[7] Ibid.

helpers and allies in securing good order."[8] He says that Christians live under God's eyes so they do what is right even without the sanction of the civil authorities. He points to the changed lives of Christians and describes Christ's teaching on marriage, love for enemies, generosity, honesty, and paying taxes.[9]

> We used to value getting wealth and possessions above all things, but now we bring what we have to a common fund and share with every one in need. We used to hate and destroy one another and were racists. But now, since the coming of Christ, we live in harmony with others of different races and pray for our enemies.[10]

The life of the early church described by Justin, the pioneering work of William Carey, and the contemporary ministry of Dr. Kiran Martin are just three examples of Christian involvement in social issues and political reform. But is social involvement a legitimate activity of Christians? Does it have biblical and theological support? This chapter sets out the case for Christian social involvement, offering three interrelated reasons: the character of God, the reign of God, and the grace of God.

1) The Character of God

The psalmist describes God in the following way:

> [He] executes justice for the oppressed,
>   who gives food to the hungry.
> The LORD sets the prisoners free;
>   the LORD opens the eyes of the blind.
> The LORD lifts up those who are bowed down;
>   the LORD loves the righteous.
> The LORD watches over the sojourners;
>   he upholds the widow and the fatherless,
>   but the way of the wicked he brings to ruin. (Ps. 146:7–9)

---

[8] Ibid., 1.12.
[9] Ibid., 1.14–17.
[10] Ibid., 1.14.

Social involvement is rooted in the character of God. He is the God who upholds the cause of the oppressed, who provides for the poor and liberates the prisoner; he sustains the marginalized and the vulnerable.

Our understanding of poverty is fundamentally related to our understanding of God. It is a question of what kind of God we worship. According to Ron Sider, concern for the poor is not "merely an ethical teaching": "it is first of all a theological truth, a central doctrine of the creed, a constantly repeated biblical teaching about the God we worship. The biblical insistence on God's concern for the poor is first of all a theological statement about the Creator and Sovereign of the universe."[11] Commenting on Deuteronomy 10:12–17 Vinoth Ramachandra says:

> Among Israel's neighbours, as indeed in the ancient cultures of the world (including Indian, Chinese, African and South American civilizations), the power of the gods was channelled through the power of certain males—the priests, kings and warriors embodied divine power. Opposition to them was tantamount to rebellion against the gods. But here, in Israel's rival vision, it is "the orphan, the widow and the stranger" with whom Yahweh takes his stand. His power is exercized in history for their empowerment.[12]

It is sometimes said that God is "biased to the poor," or people speak of his "preferential option for the poor." But such statements are open to misunderstanding. It is not that God is prejudiced in some way, still less that the poor are more deserving because of their poverty. Rather, because he is a God of justice, God opposes those who perpetrate injustice, and he sides with the victims of oppression. Vinoth Ramachandra comments: "In a sinful world where life is biased towards the wealthy and the powerful, God's actions will always be perceived as a counter-bias."[13] In situations of exploitation it is the cause of the oppressed that God upholds.

---

[11] Ronald J. Sider, *Evangelism and Social Action* (London: Hodder & Stoughton, 1993), 141.
[12] Howard Peskett and Vinoth Ramachandra, *The Message of Mission* (Nottingham, UK: Inter-Varsity, 2003), 113.
[13] Ibid., 112.

And God expects us to do the same:

Open your mouth for the mute,
   for the rights of all who are destitute.
Open your mouth, judge righteously,
   defend the rights of the poor and needy. (Prov. 31:8–9)

Take away from me the noise of your songs;
   to the melody of your harps I will not listen.
But let justice roll down like waters,
   and righteousness like an ever-flowing stream.
      (Amos 5:23–24)

To walk in the ways of the Lord, says Chris Wright, is the summary of Old Testament ethics.[14] The God who "upholds the cause of the oppressed and gives food to the hungry" expects us to walk in his ways. He expects his people to share his concern for justice. Again and again the indictment of the Old Testament prophets against God's people was both that they had turned from God to idols *and* that they had not upheld social justice (Amos 5:11–12). In Isaiah the people of God complain that God does not hear their prayers or respond to their fasting. It seems as if God is indifferent. But the problem, says Isaiah, is the indifference of the people to the cries of the poor:

"Why have we fasted, and you see it not?
   Why have we humbled ourselves, and you take no
      knowledge of it?"
Behold, in the day of your fast you seek your own pleasure,
   and oppress all your workers.
Behold, you fast only to quarrel and to fight
   and to hit with a wicked fist.
Fasting like yours this day
   will not make your voice to be heard on high.
Is such the fast that I choose,
   a day for a person to humble himself?

---

[14] Christopher J. H. Wright, *Deuteronomy*, New International Biblical Commentary (Peabody, MA: Hendrickson, 1996), 145.

Is it to bow down his head like a reed,
> and to spread sackcloth and ashes under him?
Will you call this a fast,
> and a day acceptable to the LORD?
Is not this the fast that I choose:
> to loose the bonds of wickedness,
> to undo the straps of the yoke,
to let the oppressed go free,
> and to break every yoke?
Is it not to share your bread with the hungry
> and bring the homeless poor into your house;
when you see the naked, to cover him,
> and not to hide yourself from your own flesh? (Isa. 58:3–7)

God will not hear his people when they ignore the claims of the poor (Isa. 1:10–17). The appropriate response to the God who upholds the poor is for us likewise to uphold the cause of the poor. This is the truly religious activity of those who follow the God of the Bible. This is what it means to know God. Addressing King Jehoahaz through the prophet Jeremiah, God reminds him of his father Josiah: "He judged the cause of the poor and needy; then it was well. Is not this to know me? declares the LORD" (Jer. 22:16). In a similar way James says: "Religion that is pure and undefiled before God, the Father, is this: to visit orphans and widows in their affliction, and to keep oneself unstained from the world" (James 1:27). Part of Job's argument is that he *has* cared for the poor and therefore his suffering is undeserved (Job 31:13–28).

God's concern for the poor was embodied in the Mosaic law. "I command you, 'You shall open wide your hand to your brother, to the needy and to the poor, in your land'" (Deut. 15:11). Numerous laws safeguarded both the needs and the dignity of the poor. The law of gleaning stated that landowners were to leave produce missed by the initial harvest so it could be gathered by the poor, enabling the poor to provide for themselves without being dependent on charity. Interest was not to be charged on loans to the poor so that people did not profit from their misfortune. And when a coat or millstone was taken as a guarantee for a loan, it was to be returned when it was needed. Calvin argues that the eighth commandment forbidding theft involves an obligation to assist those "we see pressed by the difficulty of affairs . . . with our abundance."[15] Jesus summed up the law as to love God and to love your neighbor as yourself (Matt. 22:34–40).

The character of God is ultimately revealed in the person of Jesus Christ. In his life he showed concern for the poor (Matt. 4:23; 9:35–38). He responded to the needy with compassionate action (Matt. 14:14; Luke 7:13). He told a rich man that he had to give everything to the poor if he wanted to follow him (Luke 12:33; 18:22), warning that "it is easier for a camel to go through the eye of a needle than for a rich person to enter the kingdom of God" (Luke 18:25). He offered acceptance to the marginalized, expressing the grace of God in his table fellowship with "sinners" (Mark 2:13–17). The poor were drawn to him just as the religious leaders were repelled by him (Luke 15:1–2). And then finally and ultimately in his death he gave us a model of love that we should extend to those in need: "By this we know love, that he laid down his life for us, and we ought to lay down our lives for the brothers. But if anyone has the world's goods and sees his brother in need, yet closes his heart against him, how does God's love abide in him?" (1 John 3:16–17).

Bob Holman, who himself resigned his post as professor of social policy at Bath University to become a community worker in Easterhouse, a deprived area of Glasgow, says of Jesus:

> His attitudes, his practices, his behaviour, were entirely in accord with the values he proclaimed. He told his disciples to be like servants—and he washed their feet. He gave the commandment to love—and he embraced the leper, the prostitute, the outcast. He told the wealthy not to put their trust in money—and he lived modestly and refused to accumulate possessions. . . . There was a loving consistence about Jesus.[16]

---

[15] John Calvin, *The Institutes of Christian Religion*, trans. F. L. Battles, ed. J. T. McNeill (Philadelphia: Westminster/SCM, 1961), 2.8.46; see also *Commentary on the Harmony of the Law*, Book 3.
[16] Cited in Forrester, *On Human Worth*, 177.

Concern for Those Outside the Christian Community

It is sometimes said that concern for the poor in the Bible is commanded only within the covenant community—whether the nation of Israel in the Old Testament or the church in the New Testament. And indeed with many texts often cited in support of social involvement, this is indeed the case. The fate of people in the parable of the sheep and the goats turns on how they have treated "the least of these"—a reference to the Christian community (see Matt. 25:31–46). Examples of the care of widows in the New Testament are within the Christian community (Acts 6:1–7; 1 Tim. 5:3–16). The command to love is focused on the people of God because we are to be a community of love reflecting the loving nature of our Father.

But our love is not to be confined to fellow Christians. The Mosaic law was given to the redeemed, covenant community, but it made specific provision in its social legislation for the care of those outside the covenant community—"the alien." Moreover, the prophets of the Old Testament condemned the injustice of other nations, while in the New Testament Paul challenged the behavior of the Roman governor Felix when he had the opportunity (Acts 24:25). We are commanded to love our neighbors (Rom. 13:9; James 2:8). And Jesus redefined love for our neighbors in the story of the good Samaritan in a way that crosses social and cultural divides to meet the one in need (Luke 10:25–37). Indeed we are commanded to love our enemies and pray for those who persecute us (Matt. 5:43–44; Luke 6:27–35; Rom. 12:17–21). Crucially, this love for others, including even the enemies of the covenant community, reflects the character of God. "He makes his sun rise on the evil and on the good" (Matt 5:45) and "He is kind to the ungrateful and the evil" (Luke 6:35). Sometimes it is said that we should only evangelize because there is little point helping someone in this life when they will face eternal death. But this ignores the example of our God who lavishes his kindness, on those destined for hell.

Human Rights and Divine Rights

The development community is increasingly making human rights, a feature of disability campaigns for some time, central to the alleviation of poverty. A rights-based approach uses the various international declarations on human rights as a tool to promote development, setting human rights as both a means to, and an end of, development. There are benefits to using the language of human rights in this way. It shifts the focus from the poor as passive recipients to the poor as people with dignity. It adds the language of justice to the language of charity. Amartya Sen, a Nobel prize–winning economist, argues for a correlation between rights and poverty. Famines are not caused by food shortages, he says, but by "entitlement failures."[17] Poverty occurs when people lack the political and legal rights to access what they need to survive. Human rights are not a luxury for the rich but essential for social development.

But do human rights provide an adequate rationale for social involvement? I suspect that the focus on human rights reflects the search for a new ethic in a post-Christian, secular world. It is an attempt to articulate afresh our moral obligation to the poor, but it roots this moral obligation in the nature of human beings. But for Christians, moral obligations are not rooted in the nature of human beings but in the nature and will of God. Our obligations are to God. He is the one with rights—not us. We have responsibilities toward God for each other. So the approach of rights-based development is godless. By that I do not mean that all human rights and all that is done in its name is contrary to the will of God—much of it does accord with God's will, and that is why we can use the instruments and language of human rights to advocate for the poor. But it must be recognized as an attempt to develop an ethic without God.

Michael Ignatieff, professor of the practice of human rights at Harvard University, says, "Human rights has become the major article of faith of a secular culture that fears it believes in nothing

---

[17] See Amartya K. Sen, *Poverty and Famines: An Essay on Entitlement and Deprivation* (Oxford, UK: Clarendon, 1981). For a brief introduction to Sen's work, see Polly Vizard, *Economic Theory, Freedom, and Human Rights: The Work of Amartya Sen*, ODI Briefing Paper (London, 2001).

else."[18] It is not enough to claim that human rights has a basis in our creation as beings in the image of God. Being made in the image of God does not mean people have an *inherent* dignity. It means they have a *relational* dignity—a dignity derived from their relationship to God as his image bearers. G. K. Chesterton said: "People are equal in the same way pennies are equal. Some are bright, others are dull; some are worn smooth, others are sharp and fresh. But all are equal in value for each penny bears the image of the sovereign, each person bears the image of the King of Kings."[19]

This, of course, does not mean that we have no obligation to one another—quite the opposite. We express our obligation to God through our care and respect of one another. The point is that when we do so, it is our obligation to God that we are expressing. Indeed, we serve God by serving other people. In the second commandment God told Israel not to worship any graven image. He did so not because God should be without images in the world, but because God already has an image in the world—humanity. We are made in God's image. We do not make graven images because God has graven an image for himself in mankind. The writer of Proverbs says: "Whoever oppresses a poor man insults his Maker, but he who is generous to the needy honors him" (Prov. 14:31). And this is also James's argument: "With [the tongue] we bless our Lord and Father, and with it we curse people who are made in the likeness of God" (James 3:9). How can we worship God with our lips and slander those made in his image? That is why we express our love for God in our love for our neighbor. The so-called horizontal and vertical dimensions are really one. To care for the poor as those made in God's image is to worship God aright.

2) The Reign of God

In the garden of Eden, God reigned over the first man and woman through his word. In our minds the idea of rule is often associated

---

[18] Michael Ignatieff, *Human Rights as Politics and Idolatry* (Princeton, NJ: Princeton University Press, 2001), 53.
[19] Cited in Forrester, *On Human Worth*, 46.

with tyranny or at least the curtailment of freedom. But the reign of God was a reign of life, freedom, peace, and joy. Under God's reign humanity enjoyed prosperity and security. Moreover, God made humanity in his image to share his reign (Gen. 1:26–28). He gave us the task of stewarding creation. We were to take the beautiful world that God had made and bring it to fulfilment. This is sometimes called the "cultural mandate." The world God made was perfect, but it was not finished. God gave it to us to explore, to enrich, to be creative. Art and science, government and business, are the outworking of the task given to us in Eden. The image of gardening captures this idea well. A good gardener works with nature, rather than against it, to create from nature something even more beautiful by tending and caring for it. In churches we often reduce the idea of stewardship to the management of money—often in the best interests of money. Good stewardship can even become synonymous with not spending money in a generous way. But the stewardship to which we were called in creation is very different. We were called to steward the world for the sake of all humanity and for the sake of creation itself. Clement of Alexandria (ca. AD 150–216) said: "Goods are called goods because they do good, and they have been provided by God for the good of humanity."[20]

But humanity rejected God's reign. We chose to live under our own authority. The result has been conflict, suffering, and injustice. Art, science, business, and government all retain their potential to honor the Creator and bless mankind, but all now also contain destructive potentials. In art we can now glorify the creation in the place of the Creator or celebrate what is wrong. More than ever we recognize the destructive potential of science alongside its benefits as we count the cost of pollution and feel the threat of advanced weaponry. Business and government take on tyrannical forms of exploitation and oppression. We thought we would be more free without God, but we became enslaved to sin, violence, and death.

---

[20] Ibid., 113.

The Bible is the story of God reestablishing his liberating reign over the world. It is the story of God restoring us in his image. Through the Lord Jesus Christ we are rescued from the punishment of sin and liberated from the power of sin. We are enabled again to be responsible coworkers with God in human society and in the stewardship of creation (e.g., 1 Tim. 6:18). The new age of liberation has begun in the midst of the old age of death so that we live in the tension between the two ages. We are being renewed, but our renewal is not yet complete, and we live in a world that is not yet renewed. In Romans 8 Paul talks about creation waiting with "eager longing for the revealing of the sons of God" (v. 19). But one day "the creation itself will be set free from its bondage to corruption and obtain the freedom of the glory of the children of God" (v. 21).

The Scope of Repentance

Jesus began his ministry by declaring that the kingdom of God is near: "Now after John was arrested, Jesus came into Galilee, proclaiming the gospel of God, and saying, 'The time is fulfilled, and the kingdom of God is at hand; repent and believe in the gospel'" (Mark 1:14–15). When that reign is proclaimed, people are called to repent. People are commanded to turn from their rejection of God and submit to his coming reign. And just as God's reign extends over every area of life, so our repentance is to affect every aspect of our lives. Our evangelism should have social consequences as we call people to repentance.

The issue of repentance has been key in evangelical debates about social involvement. In 1974, 2,500 participants from 150 countries gathered for the Lausanne Congress, officially known as the International Congress on World Evangelization. Recent years have seen evangelicals rediscover the social action for which they were well known in the eighteenth and nineteenth centuries, but which to some extent they lost in the first half of the twentieth century. And if there was one key moment when social involvement was reestablished within evangelicalism, then the Lausanne Congress was that moment. That such a representative gathering should affirm social involvement gave legitimacy and confidence to those evangelicals whose social commitments had been viewed with suspicion by their fellow evangelicals.

The key issue at Lausanne was the nature of true repentance. In the opening plenary session, John Stott argued that mission should not simply be equated with evangelism. Instead, we should speak of the total mission of the church, including both evangelism and social concern. But it was the new generation of Third World evangelicals that really set the conference alight, particularly the contributions of the Latin Americans Samuel Escobar and René Padilla. They argued that repentance is not just moral or spiritual change but a total change of life. It has social implications and these cannot be denied. At the heart of their concerns was the fear that the Congress would endorse a strategy of evangelization that would compromise the claims of discipleship for the sake of numerical results. The influence of these Third World contributors was decisive. The resulting Lausanne Covenant said, "We affirm that both evangelism and socio-political involvement are both part of our Christian duty."[21]

3) The Grace of God

As Christians we are to reflect the experience of grace that we have received. We are to be gracious because God has been gracious to us. Often, the commands of the Mosaic law were rooted in the people's experience of redemption. The Israelites, for example, were to act toward the immigrant, the vulnerable, and the poor in the light of their own experience of deliverance from slavery. The laws of gleaning were set in this context of redemption: "When you gather the grapes of your vineyard, you shall not strip it afterward. It shall be for the sojourner, the fatherless, and the widow. You shall

---

[21] From "Paragraph 5: Christian Social Responsibility," in *The Lausanne Covenant*, reproduced in *Making Christ Known: Historic Mission Documents from the Lausanne Movement 1974–1989*, ed. John Stott (Carlisle, UK: Paternoster, 1996), 24.

remember that you were a slave in the land of Egypt; therefore I command you to do this" (Deut 24:21–22). We find exactly the same reminder in the Jubilee laws that legislated for the release of slaves after seven years. The people were to act in response to their own experience of God's liberation (Deut. 15:12–15). The God who had upheld their cause expected them to uphold the cause of the oppressed.

The New Testament expects the same, and more, from those who have been rescued from their spiritual poverty and powerlessness. Consider Luke 14:

> Then Jesus said to his host, "When you give a luncheon or dinner, do not invite your friends, your brothers or relatives, or your rich neighbours; if you do, they may invite you back and so you will be repaid. But when you give a banquet, invite the poor, the crippled, the lame, the blind, and you will be blessed. Although they cannot repay you, you will be repaid at the resurrection of the righteous." (Luke 14:12–14 NIV)

The key is the phrase in verse 13: "the poor, the crippled, the lame, the blind." It is repeated in verse 21. Luke is tying together this command to welcome the poor with the parable of the great banquet in verses 15–24. In the parable God invites people to the great eternal banquet. But the rich and respectable people decline to come. Instead the good news goes out to "the poor, the crippled, the blind and the lame" (v. 21 NIV). Luke is saying that our attitude to the poor should reflect God's grace toward us. God has welcomed us to his banquet despite our poverty and powerlessness. In the same way we should welcome the poor and marginalized.

The sobering thought is this: this teaching is set in the context of a meal at the home of a Pharisee. It begins with the healing of a crippled man on the Sabbath (vv. 1–6). He is one of "the poor, the crippled, the blind and the lame" (v. 21). But for the Pharisees, their religion was more important than the needs of this man. If churches become so preoccupied with their religion that they ignore the needs of the poor, then they are in danger of becoming more like the Pharisees than like Jesus.

The next chapter of Luke's Gospel contains the stories of the lost sheep, the lost coin, and the lost son. They are wonderful stories that illustrate God's grace, God's initiative, and God's welcome in salvation. But notice the context: "Now the tax collectors and sinners were all drawing near to hear him. And the Pharisees and the scribes grumbled, saying, 'This man recives sinners and eats with them'" (Luke 15:1–2). These parables of grace are told to explain Jesus's involvement with the socially marginalized. Jesus welcomes sinners because God runs to meet repentant sinners. But the religious people mutter and complain. They are like the elder brother in the parable of the lost son who, despite his hard work for the Father, is outside the feast. Jesus leaves them facing a choice: will they join the "sinners" inside?

Our attitude to the poor, it seems, reveals a lot about our understanding of God's grace. Suppose someone says: "We should not help the poor because their situation is their own fault"—a sentiment one often hears though not usually phrased so politely. Imagine if God had said that to us. Where would we be? If we condemn the poor because of their lifestyle, then we have not understood the extent of God's grace toward *us*, with our socially respectable lifestyles that are really deeply corrupt. Gregory the Great said, "Belief in inequality arises from the spring of pride."[22] In other words, people accommodate inequality by reasoning that their wealth and privileges arise from some kind of superiority— whether skills, experience, entrepreneurial drive, national character, and so on. But grace humbles us before God. It forces us to renounce claims to superiority. The parable of the good Samaritan is addressed to a teacher of the law who asks, "Who is my neighbor?" (Luke 10:29–37). At the end we expect the answer to be: "the person we meet in need." But Jesus turns the tables on the lawyer by asking: "Which of these three, do you think, proved to

---

[22] Cited in Forrester, *On Human Worth*, 115.

be a neighbor to the man who fell among the robbers?" (v. 36). The parable places the teacher of the law not in the position of benefactor but in the position of need. The more we understand the wonderful grace of God to us in our need, the more our hearts will be open to the poor and marginalized. Often Christians wary of social involvement are persuaded not by intellectual arguments but by their own encounter with poverty. God's grace causes us to respond to need with compassion.

What Does Love Require?

Gary Haugen, the former director of the UN genocide investigation in Rwanda, presents the case for social involvement in a simple but powerful way. He presents five stories, all true cases taken up by the International Justice Mission of which he is president. Reflecting on the parable of the good Samaritan, Haugen asks us to consider in each case: "What does love require?"

> Joyti is a 14-year-old girl from a rural town in India who was abducted and drugged by four women who sold her into a brothel in Bombay. She was locked away in an underground cell and severely beaten with metal rods, plastic pipe and electrical cords until submitting to provide sex to the customers. Now she must work 7 days a week, servicing 20–40 customers a day.

> Osner is a 45-year-old man in Haiti who was illegally arrested and thrown in prison when the local mayor wanted to seize part of his land for her personal use. The detention is completely illegal under Haitian law and five different court orders have been issued demanding his release, but the prison authorities refuse to release him because of their political relationship with the mayor.

> Shama is a 10-year-old girl who was sold into bonded slavery for a family debt of $35, which was incurred to pay for her mother's medical treatment. As a result, for the last three years, Shama has been forced to work six days a week, 12–14 hours a day, rolling cigarettes by hand. She must roll 2,000 cigarettes a day or else she

gets beaten. Her bonded slavery is completely illegal under Indian law, but local authorities do not enforce the law.

Domingo is an elderly peasant farmer in Honduras who was shot in the face and leg when police illegally opened fire on him and other Lenca Indians while they were marching in the capital city for better government services in their remote region. The President of Honduras issued a promise to compensate all the injured, but nearly a year has gone by and the payments have never come. Now Domingo has lost his house and land because he is disabled and cannot work to make the payments.

Catherine is a 13-year-old girl who lives in a Manila slum and cannot go to school because her aunt forces her to work as a domestic servant. Worse, Catherine's aunt allows some of her male friends to live in the house and one of them raped Catherine while everyone else was out of the home. Catherine managed to file a complaint with the police, but the rapist is the son of a policeman and they have ignored the order to arrest the man for two years.[23]

What does love require? What does it mean for us to love Joyti, Osner, Shama, Domingo, and Catherine? Love certainly does require that the gospel be proclaimed to Joyti, to her oppressors, and to her customers. But does that exhaust our obligation of love toward her? What does love require? "Little children, let us not love in word or talk but in deed and in truth" (1 John 3:18).

Conclusion

Ron Sider tells of a prominent evangelical leader who had discovered the hundreds of Bible references on God's concern for the poor. "How, he asked me, was it possible for him to study at an evangelical college, take his theological degree at an evangelical seminary, and become a faculty member at an evangelical school and never learn about God's special concern for the poor?"[24] I once

---

[23] Gary A. Haugen, "Integral Mission and Advocacy," in *Justice, Mercy and Humility: Integral Mission and the Poor*, ed. Tim Chester (Carlisle, UK: Paternoster, 2002), 189.
[24] Sider, *Evangelism and Social Action*, 141.

read the following words to a group of students, attributing them to an unnamed radical theologian:

> Come now, you rich, weep and howl for the miseries that are coming upon you. Your riches have rotted and your garments are moth-eaten. Your gold and silver have corroded, and their corrosion will be evidence against you and will eat your flesh like fire. You have laid up treasure in the last days. Behold, the wages of the laborers who mowed your fields, which you kept back by fraud, are crying out against you, and the cries of the harvesters have reached the ears of the Lord of hosts. You have lived on the earth in luxury and in self-indulgence. You have fattened your hearts in a day of slaughter.

They were not impressed. They felt they were over the top and lacking in the sentiments of the New Testament. These words are in fact the opening verses of James 5. It illustrates the extent to which our reading of the Bible can be shaped by our context. Here was a part of the New Testament that had failed to register upon their sensibilities. Somehow they had missed it or they dismissed it as, they supposed, irrelevant to the concerns of their lives.

It illustrates, too, the extent to which our theological frameworks can shape the way we approach the text of Scripture. I remember listening to a sermon on the story of the rich man and Lazarus (Luke 16:19–31). In this parable Jesus tells the story of a rich man who lives in luxury. At his gate is Lazarus, a beggar who sits day after day dreaming of picking over the rich man's rubbish for food. When they die Lazarus is carried to Abraham's side in heaven. The rich man goes to the torment of hell from where he is able to see Lazarus at Abraham's side. He calls on Abraham to send Lazarus to cool his parched tongue, but there is a great chasm between them that cannot be crossed. Abraham says: "Child, remember that you in your lifetime received your good things, and Lazarus in like manner bad things; but now he is comforted here, and you are in anguish" (v. 25). In his concern to emphasize that salvation is all of grace, the preacher managed to deny that the parable had anything to do with wealth and poverty. They were distractions from its true meaning. As someone commented ironically to me afterwards: it was a good job we had the preacher to sort out the mess Jesus had made when he told the story!

We often see successful ministry as ministry among the affluent and successful. The models we admire are suburban models, and events are designed for university students, professionals, and white-collar families. The ministers of affluent, suburban churches dominate our conference platforms, and their patterns of church life are presented as the norm. There is little biblical reflection on poverty, because such churches are not working among the poor. Under-resourced churches struggling in marginalized areas are undervalued and their work among the poor viewed with suspicion.

Jim Wallis describes a seminary student who took an old Bible and cut out every reference to the poor with a pair of scissors. "When the seminarian was finished," says Wallis, "that old Bible hung in threads. It wouldn't hold together, it fell apart in our hands." Yet this, Wallis says, is *our* Bible—"full of holes from all we have cut out."[25] The challenge to evangelicals is not simply to maintain the inerrancy of God's Word—important as that is—but also to live by that inerrant Word.

I will let the final word go to John Owen, the great Puritan theologian:

> Churches and their members ought to think of caring for the poor as an eminent grace and excellent duty. For Christ is glorified and the gospel is honoured when we care for the poor. Many people consider it unspiritual or something that should be spontaneous rather than organized. Many think it should not be central to the work of the church. But in fact it is one of the priorities of Christian communities because it is the main way we show the gospel grace of love.[26]

---

[25] Jim Wallis, *The Soul of Politics* (New York: Fount, 1994), 163.
[26] John Owen, *True Nature of a Gospel Church*, vol. 16, *The Works of John Owen* (Edinburgh: Banner of Truth, 1968), 144. I have rephrased Owen's original language in more contemporary English. The original quote is: "It were well if all churches, and all the members of them, would wisely consider how eminent is this grace, how excellent is this duty, of making provision for the poor—

Summary

From the time of the early church onwards, Christians have cared for the poor. We are called to this because of:

- *the character of God*—the Bible speaks of God as the God of the poor who upholds the cause of the oppressed. He commands us to do likewise throughout the Scriptures and through the example of Christ;
- *the reign of God*—humanity was made to share God's loving reign over the creation, stewarding the earth's resources for the good of all and for the good of creation itself. In the gospel we are called to repentance, to resubmit to the reign of God in every area of life;
- *the grace of God*—we are to show love to others, especially the marginalized, in a way that reflects our experience of God's grace.

We are to have a special concern for our fellow Christians, for the Christian community is called to witness to life under God's rule. But we are also to have concern for our neighbors in the wider society in the same way that God "makes his sun rise on the evil and on the good" (Matt. 5:45).

Returning to our characters from the introduction, we have seen in this chapter the strength of Catherine's position. There is a strong biblical case for Christian social involvement rooted in the character of God, the call to repentance, and our experience of God's grace in Christ. In the next chapter we will develop this by countering the suggestion that Christianity is a private affair.

---

how much the glory of Christ and honour of the gospel are concerned herein; for whereas, for the most part, it is looked on as an ordinary work, to be performed transiently and cursorily, scarce deserving any of the time which is allotted unto the church's public service and duties, it is indeed one of the most eminent duties of Christian societies, wherein the principal exercise of the second evangelical grace, namely, love, doth consist."

2

More Than a Private Faith

Many Christians believe that we should not get involved in the business of politics. Christianity is a private, personal matter, they argue. It does not and should not speak to social issues. The task of the church is to create and foster personal faith. Moreover, it is not just some Christians who are wary of Christian involvement in society; society itself is often wary of Christian faith intruding into politics. Writing in *the Times* of a British context, Michael Gove says:

> The British have become uneasy with public protestations of private religious belief, doubly so when the language of faith is entangled with the practice of politics. The Prime Minister's own closest advisers believe that any overt religiosity on Mr Blair's behalf is dangerous. When the Prime Minister was asked about his faith by a reporter . . . [his official spokesman] cut in to insist: "We don't do God.". . . In the party which once owed more to Methodism than Marxism it is now the love of God that dare not speak its name.[1]

How did we get to this situation? It was not always like this, nor is it like this in many parts of the world today. Jesus died in fulfillment of God's eternal plan of salvation, but the immediate his-

---

[1] Michael Gove, "Thank God for politicians who take their cue from above," *London Times*, May 6, 2003.

torical reason for his execution was that he was considered by both the Jewish and the Roman authorities as a threat to the social and political order (John 11:48; 19:12). Paul wrote that we should submit to the governing authorities (Rom. 13:1), but he himself spent much of his life in state prisons for his activities. His was no private faith but one that "turned the world upside down" (Acts 17:6). In Revelation 18 John denounces the economic system of the Roman Empire, calling upon the churches in Asia Minor to "come out of her" (Rev. 18:4). The apostolic writers did not call upon the church to engage in armed resistance or pursue political power. But describing the dragon and its two beasts—the political power of empire and its underlying ideology—John commends those who "have conquered him by the blood of the Lamb and by the word of their testimony, for they loved not their lives even unto death" (Rev. 12:11).

John Calvin, the Protestant Reformer, did not see Christianity as a private affair, getting involved in the public administration of Geneva—even when that included the sewerage system! The Reformed theologian Abraham Kuyper became prime minister of Holland and founded two newspapers. Thomas Chalmers, the nineteenth-century Scottish church leader and theologian, pioneered parish ministry among the poor. In England Elizabeth Fry campaigned for prison reform, and the great Victorian preacher Charles Haddon Spurgeon founded an orphanage, along with other charitable works. James Montgomery, the writer of the hymns "Hail to the Lord's Anointed" and "Angels from the Realms of Glory," was a campaigning newspaper editor in Sheffield, twice imprisoned for his political views. William Wilberforce successfully campaigned as a parliamentarian for the abolition of the slave trade. The Earl of Shaftsbury advocated the cause of working children and the mentally ill while dedicating himself to social work in slums and foreign missions. The founders of the Salvation Army, William and Catherine Booth, started a range of social work among the poor of London and beyond, and William Booth wrote the controversial book *In Darkest England*, calling the nation to face up to the challenge of poverty. Bishop David Gitari assigned development workers and evangelists in each parish in his Kenyan diocese, resulting in economic development and rapid church planting. At the same time he has been outspoken in his condemnation of political corruption and economic injustice, even after an attempt was made on his life in 1989. Frank Chikane, a Pentecostal pastor from South Africa, was tortured for six weeks because of his opposition to apartheid. For these people, and many more whose stories will only be properly celebrated in eternity, their Christian faith was a public affair with social implications.

1) How Do We Know What Is True?

To discover why so many people view Christianity as a private and personal affair without social implications, we must retrace the story of Western thought.

Divine Revelation

Consider the question, "How do we know what is true?" In medieval times the answer was straightforward: we believe what we have always believed. Tradition defined what we know. And for people in western Europe, that tradition was mediated through the Roman Catholic Church. But the central role of tradition in determining what we know to be true was challenged by the Reformation. One of the Reformation's great principles was *sola scriptura*, "Scripture alone." Martin Luther, John Calvin, and the other leaders of the Reformation made revelation central. To the question, "How do we know what is true?" they answered: "What has been revealed by God." *Sola scriptura* did not mean Scripture was the only source of theology. The Reformers quoted past theologians freely as authoritative guides. They reflected on experience and used their reason. What they meant was that Scripture was the supreme authority. And in particular it was the supreme authority in contrast with the authority of the church and its traditions. The Catholic Church claimed the right to interpret the Scriptures; it was the Scriptures together with the interpretation of the church that carried authority. And it was to this that the Reformers raised the challenge of *sola scriptura*.

But how then were people to decide between competing interpretations of the Bible? The Catholic answer was, as always, that the hierarchy of the church should decide. The church, and especially the pope, was the ultimate authority. But when the Reformation demonstrated that the church could get its theology wrong, it delivered a fatal blow. This, at a time when its political power was on the wane, destroyed the hegemony of the Catholic Church. Who now could determine whose interpretation was correct?

The Anabaptists' response was to say that the community of believers determines together the interpretation of Scripture. The Anabaptists were the radical wing of the Reformation, rejecting the idea of a state church and seeing the church instead as a gathering of believers. They held that the gathered believers could understand the Scriptures. The Anabaptists spoke of "the Rule of Paul," a reference to 1 Corinthians 14:29: "Let two or three prophets speak, and let the others weigh what is said" (1 Cor. 14:29). When debates arose they called on the believing community to decide who speaks more clearly the truth of the Scripture. This "community hermeneutic" is closely related to what the Anabaptists called "the hermeneutics of obedience." The Anabaptists argued that there was a close relationship between understanding the Bible and obedience to its demands; between knowledge and discipleship. The impediment to knowledge of God is not ignorance but sin. Anabaptists like Hans Denck and Hans Hut used to say that true knowledge of God cannot be achieved simply from reading the Bible. Denck said, "No man can know Christ unless he follows after him in life." The readiness to obey Christ's words is a prerequisite to understanding them. And because there was no understanding without obedience, so a disciplining community was necessary for the proper interpretation of the Bible.[2]

---

[2] Willard Swartley, ed., *Essays on Biblical Interpretation: Anabaptist-Mennonite Perspectives* (Elkhart, IN: Institute of Mennonite Studies, 1984); and Eddie Johnston, "Biblical Interpretation and the Church," *Searching Together* (Spring 1980): 21–31.

But the dominant approach in Protestantism focused on the individual. The Reformers argued that every believer is a priest with access to God through Christ. Unlike the Anabaptists, however, they saw this in individual terms. In other words, when it comes to competing interpretations of Scripture, every individual believer can decide for himself. It accorded each person a role in determining truth. It was no longer the institutions of the church that determined truth but every believer enlightened by the Spirit.

The result of this shift was a series of religious wars in which truth was quite literally fought over. This led to a search for a nonreligious foundation for social morals—ethics detached from theological roots. Theology was no longer expected to make universal claims, certainly not in the public realm. Instead it was confined to the domestic realm. Hugo Grotius (1583–1645), although himself a Christian, argued that public morality should be conducted *etsi Deus non daretur*, "as if God did not exist." This was not atheism but an attempt to find a foundation for public life instead of the fragmented foundation of religion. Individual religious conviction was separated from public morality.

At the same time the Renaissance had led to an explosion of learning, fueled by the printing press. There were radical new developments in science led by the work of Isaac Newton. All of these gave new urgency to the questions, "How can we know what is true?" and "How can I know the truth about God?" In response, philosophers like René Descartes (1596–1650) began to argue that the existence of God could be established using human reason.

Human Reason

Have you ever thought that maybe life is all a big dream? Could it be that there is no God, no self, and no world? This was one of the problems that exercised René Descartes. Descartes decided that we can no longer start with faith as a presupposition. We must doubt everything until we can be sure we truly know something. Descartes was musing away at this when he famously cried: *cogito ergo sum:* "I think therefore I am." The very act of doubting was evidence of existence, because only an existing being can think and doubt. From there Descartes believed we could establish the existence of God and the natural world.

It sounds good, but it represented a decisive and fatal move. Human reason had become the judge of what was true. It seems reasonable to us that God exists—therefore, he does. But what if it seems reasonable that God does not exist? When it came to revelation, reason was no longer a tool to assist our understanding of the Bible. Reason was the ultimate purveyor of truth. No longer would revelation judge human reason. Human reason would now judge revelation. And so the so-called higher biblical criticism was born, which gradually removed from the Bible any unity, historicity, reliability, and authority. The result within the church was theological liberalism. The result outside of the church was atheism.

Though there were antecedents, Descartes is usually seen as the father of the Enlightenment. People talk about "the Cartesian revolution" ("Cartesian" from Des*cartes*). The Enlightenment was defined by Emmanuel Kant as "the spirit's determination to exercise its intellectual faculties with unfettered integrity." It is described as "the age of reason." It was this approach to philosophy, together with the industrial revolution, the rise of capitalism, and the growth of urbanization, that shaped modernity—the modern worldview. The hope of modernism was that through shared human reason, humanity could agree on what was true. Through a process of rational enquiry we could find a shared basis for human society. Postmodernism rightly rebels against this false hope. Human reason is corrupted by sin. In postmodern terms, truth is a function of power. Claims to absolute truth are often used by the powerful to maintain their position of power.

Human Experience

Not everyone was happy with the central place given to human reason. The Romantic movement felt that this scientism and rationalism were too mechanistic, ignoring the emotions of the human spirit. William Blake (1757–1827) rejected the mechanical world of rationalism and of industrialization (the "dark Satanic Mills" of his famous poem *Jerusalem*). He appealed instead to man's aesthetic and spiritual sensitivities. William Wordsworth (1770–1850) saw nature as the theater in which one can sense God, while Samuel Taylor Coleridge (1772–1834) condemned attempts to construct rational proofs for the existence of God. It is no accident that all three are primarily known as poets. Poetic discourse rather than rational discourse was a better medium for conveying profound truth. Coleridge was the most influential of these poets on wider philosophy and thought. Coleridge was addicted to opium and believed it brought him deep spiritual insight. He said: "All revelation is *ab intra*" (from within). He called adherents to the doctrine of the inspiration of Scripture "orthodox liars for God." Instead we receive truth from the Bible when "whatever finds me bears witness for itself that it had proceeded from a Holy Spirit." In other words, our spiritual sensibilities recognize truth when they encounter it—whether that truth is from the Bible or from drug-induced ecstasy.

The main representative of Romanticism within theology is the nineteenth-century theologian Friedrich Schleiermacher (1768–1834). Schleiermacher was heavily influenced by pietism in his early life, and he believed that theology should be rooted in the piety of the church. Schleiermacher defined God as our sense of absolute dependence. Self-consciousness is consciousness of dependence and therefore of God. Jesus is the archetype of God-consciousness. Our impoverished God-consciousness is renewed through the God-consciousness of Jesus.

2) Public Truth and Private Faith

Romanticism is in some ways a reaction to the rationalism of the Enlightenment. It turns from a mechanistic view of reality to a more spiritual view. While rationalism focuses the search for certainty in human reason, Romanticism focuses on human experience. And yet Romanticism is still very much part of the Enlightenment. It does not replace reason but creates a separate private sphere for spiritual truth. Human reason still dominated the public realms of politics, science, and economics, whereas Romanticism secured a place for spiritual things within the realm of personal beliefs and values.

These intellectual changes were reinforced by social changes. Before the industrial revolution most people lived and worked at the same location, often in the same building. Private life and public life were one. But the industrial revolution and increased urbanization radically changed this. The factory replaced the household as the place of work. The public world of work and the private world of the home began to gain their own codes of conduct; the former dominated by men, the latter by women. A friend of mine, who lived in a cottage in the Yorkshire Dales over a mile from the nearest house, visited London and found it a lonely place. Living in a rural context, for him the private and public still cohered. Lives were shared and open. But how can you share your life with the millions of urban dwellers who surround you every day? Instead the home becomes a haven, a place of refuge from the constant proximity of people. We invented "privacy." And so my friend found staying in a London block of flats whose inhabitants avoided contact a lonely experience. A split between the public and private spheres with differing codes of conduct and values has become part of the mechanisms by which we cope with postindustrial, urban life.

Imagine you had just turned on the television. You have one of those old television sets that takes a moment or two to warm up so that the sound comes before you see the picture. And you hear the words, "Jesus is Lord." What kind of an image would you expect to see? An interview with a government minister explaining the factors that have shaped government policy? A businessman explaining his company's strategy? A world leader discussing international affairs? An arts program assessing a recent novel? I guess that you would be surprised if any of these pictures came into view. In all these contexts the words "Jesus is Lord" sound out of place.

In modern thinking, public truth and private faith have become polarized. Public truth means the truth we operate with in public life: in politics, the media, education, science, and culture. In public discourse God-talk has no place. The lordship of Christ is not allowed to have any bearing on public truth. Public truth must be observable and verifiable. Faith and values are relegated to one's private life. You can hold beliefs in God, but you must not let them intrude into public life. They are private. Opinion polls show that the majority of people believe in God, but our society is resistant to the intrusion of religion in public life. God may be in heaven, but we do not want him meddling down here on earth. The only truth that can be commended universally is truth based on reason and observation.

Evangelicalism in the twentieth century latched onto this space for private faith. Much Christian scholarship moved toward liberalism under the influence of rationalism. This left evangelicalism without the intellectual resources to withstand the assault of modernist thinking. Instead it retreated into the private sphere that modernity allowed for it. Evangelicals practiced their religion and maintained their orthodoxy within their own circles. But they no longer engaged with public truth. They no longer asserted the gospel as public truth, as truth relevant to politics, economics, or science. People often refer to this attitude as "pietism." In fact historically "pietism" started life as a quite proper emphasis on personal devotion. But with the modern split between public truth and private values, pietism became *just* personal devotion. It was the safe option—to live within a ghetto unaffected and unchallenged by the world. But its missiological consequences have been far-reaching. And its effects are with us to this day.

At the last general election in the United Kingdom, I compared the guides for voters circulated by a variety of Christian organizations. A number focused almost exclusively on issues of personal morality without reference to economic or social justice. The underlying assumption was that issues of personal and family morality are "Christian" issues but that the gospel has nothing to say about economic justice. Other Christians go further, advocating noninvolvement in politics. The assumption is the same: that the gospel has nothing to say about economics or politics, only about personal faith. This can even mean that Christians operate with two sets of values: the public values of the market and the private values of compassion. In their private lives they are generous and caring, contributors to charitable causes, and are model family members. But in the public world of business and politics they self-consciously rule out compassion as a factor in making decisions that are instead governed by the rules of the market.

Or consider another example: I was talking to a local coordinator of the Religious and Theological Students' Fellowship (RTSF), which helps students think through the challenges to biblical faith posed by their theological studies, and he despaired at the apathy of evangelical students toward these challenges. The courses in which they were involved were undermining biblical revelation and eroding their confidence in the truth. But most students coped by living in two worlds. They participated in their studies like any other students while enthusiastically enjoying church on Sundays. Some could not even recognize the conflicts. Others recognized that their lecturers were undermining the truths of Christianity, but instead of engaging with the issues, they sought comfort through the rather shakier foundations of the buzz they enjoyed on Sundays. The public truth of the university was divorced from the private truth of their religious experience.

In 1986 Yoweri Museveni became president of Uganda when his National Resistance Army overthrew the military government. As a teenager Museveni had attended Scripture Union youth camps. On one occasion, with civil war raging in neighboring Tanzania, Museveni suggested to the camp leaders that they devote the camp prayers that evening to intercession for this conflict. He was told: "We don't concern ourselves with things like that." The prayers went ahead with the focus on the needs of the camp and the spiritual well-being of its participants. It was a decisive moment in Museveni's life. If Christianity had nothing to say to the issues of the day, then he would look elsewhere for his guiding philosophy.

In 1994 an estimated one million people were killed in Rwanda in brutal ethnic violence. Whether the differences between the main ethnic groups, the Hutus and the Tutsis, are racial or social are disputed. But whatever their origins, they were not a problem until the colonial era when first the Germans and then the Belgians used the Tutsi minority to rule the country. After independence Hutus increasingly took power, with the leaders manipulating racial differences to consolidate their power. In April 1994 the plane carrying the Rwandan president was shot down. Within one hour roadblocks had been set up on all the roads leading out of the capital Kigali. Tutsis, together with sympathetic Hutus, were being butchered by Hutu militia, incited by the broadcasts of Rwandan radio.

Yet Rwanda was one of the most evangelized countries in Africa. It had known revival, and over 80 percent of the population claimed to be Christians. How could such a "Christian" country be responsible for such widespread and horrific violence? Part of the answer may be that the church placed self-interest above wider issues of reconciliation and social justice. An often heard refrain in Rwanda used of the church is, "If someone puts food in your mouth, then you're not free to speak out."[3]

But part of the answer also lies in the revival that Rwanda experienced. In the 1930s much of East Africa experienced a period of revival, characterized by conviction of sin, public confession, and witness. The revival started in Uganda but spread as far as South Africa, Kenya, Tanzania, Burundi, and Congo. It was a strong influence in Rwanda. At its best the East African Revival confronted ethnic issues. One of the favorite sayings of the revival was, "The

---

[3] Dewi A. Hughes with Matthew Bennett, *God of the Poor: A Biblical Vision of God's Present Rule* (Carlisle, UK: OM, 1998), 232.

ground is level at the cross." And it also encouraged Africans to challenge the racist attitudes of the white missionaries.

But the teaching of the church, shaped by the East African Revival, was narrowly pietistic. "One of the problems," according to Emmanuel Kolini, of the diocese of Shoba in Zaire, "was lack of teaching on how the Scriptures could be applied to social and practical questions."[4] The church failed to teach the implications of Christ's lordship over all of life. It focused upon blessing, experience, and "spiritual" concerns, when, according to Roger Bowen of Mid-Africa Ministry (formerly the Rwanda Mission), there was a need to teach "the whole counsel of God" with "teaching on how to live out Christian discipleship in the secular world."[5] Alan Nichols of World Vision Australia asks: "In the light of Rwanda, the most Christian nation in Africa, blowing up the way it did, does this reflect on Christian missionaries from the West offering 'cheap grace' which has not actually converted racial bias, the feelings of ethnic superiority, or the long-held grudges of one people against another?"[6]

One example of the failure to give fuller biblical teaching was in the area of sin. Ironically, while the movement placed a high emphasis upon confession of sin, it had only a limited doctrine of sin. It confined sin to private morality—lying, drinking, smoking, and adultery—with "little awareness of the solidarities of sin that we are embedded in as members of society."[7] With no understanding of social evils or corporate sins, there was an often naïve support for those in power, regardless of their actions. According to to Bowen, missionaries preached a form of "pietism" that encouraged the "withdrawal from the public life of the nation or a naïve uncritical support of the party in power."[8] And Emmanuel Kolini says, "Some missionaries taught that politics was a dirty game and

---

[4] Cited in John Martin, "Rwanda: Why?," *Transformation* 12:2 (1995): 2.
[5] Roger Bowen, "Revivalism and Ethnic Conflict: Questions from Rwanda," *Transformation* 12:2 (1995): 17.
[6] Cited in Martin, "Rwanda: Why?," 2.
[7] Bowen, "Revivalism and Ethnic Conflict," 17.
[8] Cited in Hughes, *God of the Poor*, 232.

the Christian duty was to escape it."[9] An edition of the journal *Transformation* devoted to the lessons of Rwanda comments:

> The worldwide church should be deeply concerned: not just in their compassion for suffering on the part of its fellow human beings, but as a warning to itself. There must have been serious inadequacies and failings in the theology and spirituality of the church in Rwanda if the East African Revival and mission legacy could prove so weak. Other churches should take very seriously the dramatic breakdown of Christianity and evangelism under pressure.[10]

3) Jesus, the Lord of Every Area of Human Life

At its heart the issue has to do with the lordship of Christ. The Bible claims that Jesus is Lord over all things:

> He is the image of the invisible God, the firstborn of all creation. For by him all things were created, in heaven and on earth, visible and invisible, whether thrones or dominions or rulers or authorities—all things were created through him and for him. And he is before all things, and in him all things hold together. And he is the head of the body, the church. He is the beginning, the firstborn from the dead, that in everything he might be preeminent. For in him all the fullness of God was pleased to dwell, and through him to reconcile to himself all things, whether on earth or in heaven, making peace by the blood of his cross. (Col. 1:15–20)

Jesus is Lord as creator, for through him all things were created—including thrones, powers, rulers, and authorities. And Jesus is Lord as redeemer, for it is God's purpose through Christ to reconcile all things: "to unite all things in him, things in heaven and things on earth" (Eph. 1:10). Every area of human life is under his authority. Abraham Kuyper said: "There is not a square inch in the whole domain of our human existence over which Christ,

---

[9] Cited in Martin, "Rwanda: Why?," 2.
[10] Editorial Comment, *Transformation* 12:2 (1995): 1.

who is Sovereign over *all*, does not say 'Mine.'"[11] That authority is ignored and resisted all around us because humanity has rejected God's reign. But one day Christ will return, and God's glory will fill the earth as the waters cover the sea. In the meantime, the Christian community is the place where the reign of God is being reestablished. Christians are those people who now acknowledge the lordship of Christ. So the work of bringing all things under the reign of God has begun even now in the church over which Christ is the head. The church is the vanguard of the new creation, the "area" of the world in which God's liberating reign is already acknowledged and enjoyed, so that in everything Christ might have the supremacy.

This means that Christians should live under the authority of Christ in *all* dimensions of life—in social life as well as family life, in political and economic relationships, as well as in personal morality. In the New Testament the scope of true repentance extends to social affairs. This includes both care of other Christians within the believing community and concern for our neighbor in the wider society. John the Baptist fleshes out repentance as sharing your clothing with those who have none. He tells tax collectors and soldiers to stop their extortion (Luke 3:7–14). Jesus says that salvation has come to Zacchaeus as Zacchaeus demonstrates that the gospel has transformed his economic relationships (Luke 19:8–10). God's purpose in salvation is that we might "do good works, which God prepared in advance for us to do" (Eph. 2:10). Saving faith proves itself in a commitment to the needs of others (James 2:14–26).

This does not mean proof-texting. It has always been my policy to avoid adding Bible references to policy documents, because it encourages people to think that a few isolated Bible verses make a position biblical. Instead we need to think through issues in terms of the Bible's big story—a biblical worldview. Our social involvement should be set in the framework of a biblical world-

---

[11] Cited in Howard Peskett and Vinoth Ramachandra, *The Message of Mission* (Nottingham, UK: Inter-Varsity, 2003), 29.

view shaped by the story of redemption. We should explore issues by looking at them in the light of creation, humanity's fall into sin, God's redemption—promised in the Old Testament and accomplished through Christ—and the return of Christ and the transformation of all things. Being biblical, then, means ensuring that our actions are related to our biblical framework rather than appending isolated biblical texts to each action.

It is sometimes said that evangelism is the best way to change a society, and there is a lot of truth in this. But, as Melba Maggay points out, "experience shows that having more Christians does not necessarily ensure a just society." She cites two reasons. First, "people may experience saving faith, but may not necessarily move towards the far-reaching social implications of that faith, either due to lack of understanding or to a failure to obey." Second, society is too complex to be changed by personal obedience and good will. "There are entrenched powers and monstrous structures we need to address and contend with."[12] She concludes:

> To speak of Jesus as Lord is to demand subjection of personal and social life under his kingly rule. To call for repentance is to ask people to turn away, not simply from their individual vices, but from participation in the collective guilt of organized injustice. To invite people to come in faith is to challenge them to walk in trusting obedience, to know God in the agony of commitment and concrete engagement in the life of the world.[13]

Summary

Many people assume religion is a private affair that should have nothing to do with public issues. During the Enlightenment human reason became the basis of public debate in the hope that it might provide a basis for shared social convictions. Religious faith was confined to the private realm. Threatened by the Enlightenment assault on their beliefs, Christians often chose to operate

---

[12] Melba Maggay, *Transforming Society* (Oxford, UK: Regnum, 1994), 16.
[13] Ibid., 20.

within the private sphere that the modern world allowed them. But Jesus is the Lord of every area of human life. Our faith should shape our involvement in social and cultural issues.

Chapters 1 and 2 have presented the case for Christian social involvement, the standpoint represented by Catherine in the introduction. In the next chapter we will see the strength of Douglas's position and the validity of his concerns. The chapter shows why the proclamation of the gospel message must be central to Christian social involvement.

The Case for Evangelizing the Poor

What is the greatest need of people in your area? Your answer might depend on where you live. Some of the needs we face in the area that my church serves are racism, poor mental health, and unemployment. In leafier suburbs the problems may be less evident, but behind the curtains of the large houses are people facing loneliness, domestic violence, emptiness, and household debt. In the shanty towns and slums of the Third World the need is for clean water, proper sanitation, housing, education, regular income, and basic health care. I remember asking the women of a slum in New Delhi about their hopes for the future. The thing they wanted most was electricity. They wanted to be able to run fans to make the heat of the slums more bearable. A few weeks later the temperature soared close to 120 degrees and a number of people in the slum died of heat exhaustion.

A 2011 Gallup Poll showed that Americans think the number-one problem facing the nation is unemployment followed by the economy in general.[1] What would your friends and neighbors regard as the big local needs? Healthcare? Immigration? Crime? Or what about at an international level? The environment? Poverty? Terrorism?

---

[1] http://www.gallup.com/poll/149453/Unemployment-Emerges-Important-Problem.aspx.

Looking at the world around us, we might well agree with these answers. But the Bible opens ours eyes to a much broader horizon. It reveals that people have a need much greater than any mentioned above and of which people are largely unaware—the need to be reconciled to God and so escape his wrath.

1) The Priority of the Future

As we think about issues of social need and social involvement, the place to start is at the end. We need to begin by considering the end of history. The Bible is a story that is heading toward a climax when Christ returns to judge the living and the dead. The Bible story is built on the belief that the future that God promises is better than the present we currently experience. Paul says, "I consider that the sufferings of this present time are not worth comparing with the glory that is to be revealed to us" (Rom. 8:18). He goes on to argue that we, like creation, groan as we wait for the future glory because our redemption is in the future. We do not yet have that for which we hope. Indeed, it makes no sense to talk about Christian hope, Paul argues, unless we are waiting for the fullness of salvation in the future (Rom. 8:22–25). If resurrection has already taken place in some spiritual sense, then all that we believe and all that we do is in vain (1 Cor. 15:12–18).

The whole of the Bible story reflects this perspective. It is not a question of a few texts that speak about the return of Christ. The whole biblical narrative is moving toward fulfilment in the new creation. The heroes of the Old Testament described in Hebrews 11 are all commended because they were looking forward. We think of it as a chapter about faith, but the writer begins the chapter by defining faith in terms of hope: "Now faith is the assurance of things hoped for, the conviction of things not seen" (Heb. 11:1). What makes them an example to us is that they made the future, promised by God, a priority over this life. Consider Moses: "By faith Moses, when he was grown up, refused to be called the son of Pharaoh's daughter, choosing rather to be mistreated with the people of God than to enjoy the fleeting pleasures of sin. He considered the reproach of Christ greather wealth than the treasures of Egypt, for he was looking to the reward" (Heb. 11:24–26). Moses is commended because he made the future promised by God a greater priority than enjoyment in the present. He was looking ahead to his reward. Ultimately Jesus himself is our supreme example. This section in Hebrews ends: "Let us fix our eyes on Jesus, the author and perfecter of our faith, who for the joy set before him endured the cross, scorning its shame, and sat down at the right hand of the throne of God" (Heb. 12:2 NIV).

In summary: blessing in God's future is more important than blessing in this life. And this is exactly what Jesus himself says: "Do not lay up for yourselves treasures on earth, where moth and rust destroy and where thieves break in and steal, but lay up for yourselves treasures in heaven, where neither moth nor rust destroys and where thieves do not break in and steal" (Matt. 6:19–20).

In Matthew 18:8 Jesus says: "If your hand or your foot causes you to sin, cut it off and throw it away. It is better for you to enter life crippled or lame than with two hands or two feet to be thrown into the eternal fire." It is better to be maimed in this life and enter heaven than to be healthy in this life and spend eternity in hell. In the same way, we need to say without embarrassment that it is better if someone is converted but remains poor than if he becomes healthy and wealthy but remains unconverted. John Hooper, a Protestant during the reign of Mary Tudor, was facing martyrdom when he was urged by a friend to renounce the faith. "Life is sweet, death is bitter," his friend told him. Hooper replied: "Eternal life is more sweet, eternal death is more bitter."

Sometimes such a focus on the future is dismissed as dualism, but that is a mistake. Dualism has become something of a bogey word that is used to dismiss arguments without a true engagement with the issues. Properly speaking, dualism is the belief that the spiritual is good or important while the material is bad or unimportant. Paul calls this the doctrine of demons (1 Tim. 4:1). Some in Ephesus where Timothy was working denigrated sex and food.

They claimed that women should leave behind the responsibilities of motherhood and pursue a higher, more spiritual calling (1 Tim. 2:15). But Paul says these things are good gifts from God. We can be spiritual people in marriage, in the home, and so on. To be spiritual is to walk in step with the Spirit in every area of life. It is not to live on some ethereal plane. Dualists see salvation in terms of the soul escaping the prison of the body. But Christian theology, in contrast, affirms that salvation involves the resurrection of the body. We are right to oppose such dualism.

But to say that physical and spiritual belong together is very different from saying that the temporal is as important as the eternal. The Bible consistently says we should make the eternal future our priority. In Matthew 10:28 we read: "Do not fear those who kill the body but cannot kill the soul." Is that dualism? Is this saying that the soul is more important than the body? If it is, then it is Jesus who says it. But in fact Jesus goes on: "Rather fear him who can destroy both soul and body in hell" (Matt. 10:28). The issue is not whether the soul is more important than the body. Jesus says we should be concerned for both soul *and* body. The issue is that our eternal fate is more important than what happens to us in this life.

2) The Need for Reconciliation with God through Jesus Christ

We see all sorts of need around us. They are immediate and evident. But the priority of the eternal future means that the greatest need for all of us is to be reconciled to God and so escape his wrath. And this is the greatest need of the poor. I remember hearing a Christian who had worked among the famine victims of the Biafra conflict in Nigeria in the late 1960s. He spoke of how their greatest concern as they faced death was to be told about life after death. People often say rather glibly, "Hungry stomachs don't have ears." But the hungry stomachs of the Biafrans were all ears for good news in the face of death. Jim Wallis describes a consultation between church leaders and gang members from urban America. "They virtually pleaded with us," he relates, "saying, 'We've been trying to find God for so long.'" When one of the pastors asked what the church could do for them, they replied: "Help us find a relationship to God. We need our churches to lead us to the Lord."[2]

The Bible is clear: we are all alienated from God—young and old, white and black, male and female, rich and poor. Paul talks about us as God's enemies. It is not just that we have become God's enemies. God has become our enemy. Our sin has broken the relationship with God for which we were made. It has placed us in opposition to God. We want to be gods of our own lives in rebellion against God. And God would not be God if he ignored this rebellion. He would not be just if he ignored the pain and suffering that it causes. He would not be worth worshiping if he was indifferent to evil and inhumanity. So the biggest problem we all face is God's judgment. Our greatest need is to be reconciled with God. But God in his love and grace has sent his own Son to die in our place, to take our punishment, to pay our debt. So we can be reconciled to God and we can escape his wrath through Jesus Christ.

Moving beyond Felt Needs

This is familiar territory to most of us, but we need to be clear about its implications. It means it is never enough to address people's felt needs. Felt needs can be a good starting point because the gospel addresses the human condition in all its complexity. But we need to move beyond people's felt needs. Nobody articulates God's judgment as a felt need. Indeed people are blind to the need to escape God's judgment—the need that is, in fact, their greatest need. Sometimes something happens that awakens people to the reality of judgment, but it is rare for people to ask how they can escape God's judgment without the Spirit's using the gospel message to open their eyes to that need.

A community development project in Honduras was working with indigenous people in the rainforest. The communities

---

[2] Jim Wallis, *The Soul of Politics* (New York: Fount, 1994), 19.

felt their greatest need was for education. But the development agency knew that loggers were progressively clearing the forest. If nothing was done, the land and the livelihood of the communities would be threatened. The community had no awareness of this. So the development agency took them upstream to show them what was happening. They then began to work together on claiming land rights and establishing a reserve. Their need for education was a real need. But they had to be shown that they faced a much greater need.

It is like that with God's judgment. People think they have all sorts of needs, and often they are real and pressing needs. But there is a much greater need of which people are unaware. It is our job to take them upstream, as it were, and warn them of the coming judgment of God. We cannot wait for people to express the need for reconciliation with God. Apart from the gospel, we have enough trouble acknowledging we are sinners, let alone acknowledging that we deserve the judgment of God.

Without an ongoing awareness of eternal needs, over time our focus will become temporal needs. A community's temporal needs press themselves upon us. They are, by definition, immediate. We need consciously, therefore, to keep in mind the greatest need that is known to us only through the gospel—the need of a person to be reconciled with God and escape his wrath. Time and again this has proved the greatest challenge facing Christian social involvement—to keep in view the greatest gift we have to offer a needy world: the words of eternal life.

God made humanity in his image to rule over, and care for, creation. We were made to reflect the creativity of God in art and science. When we paint, write, investigate, sing, explore, and create, we are doing that for which we were made. God placed us in the world to enjoy his creation and in so doing to give him glory. And we were made to reflect the love of God. The God who is a relational being made us to enjoy a relationship with him and with one another. We were made to care for one another. The image of God has been marred by human rebellion against God, but God is restoring that image in us through Christ. This means that Christian involvement in culture and society is good and right. To enjoy God's world and to share its blessings is that for which we were* made. Such activities require no further justification than this. They are valid in their own right.

But the world is not as God made it. People are no longer in relationship with God. As valid as cultural and social involvement are in their own right, they cannot be seen in isolation from the task of reconciling people to God through the gospel. In other words, the doctrine of creation means cultural and social involvement are valid, but the doctrine of sin and the offer of salvation mean that to engage in culture and creativity without evangelism is indulgent. To engage in social action without evangelism is to ⟩ fail the people we profess to love. I may play in a music band or be a member of a sports team or run a homeless project. Such activities are justified by the creation mandate. But I cannot engage in those activities without also wanting to share the good news with the people I meet through those activities.

3) The Centrality of Proclamation

In 1 Corinthians 1:18 Paul says: "The word of the cross is folly to those who are perishing, but to us who are being saved it is the power of God" (1 Cor. 1:18). It is easy to miss the surprising nature of this statement. What is the power of God? How are we saved from God's judgment? How are we reconciled to God? Paul does not say that the cross is the power of God, as we might expect. He says that the *message* of the cross is the power of God. It is, literally, "the word of the cross." God's power and Christ's saving work are present through God's Word. So if the priority of the future drives us to seek the reconciliation of people with God through the cross of Christ, then this in turn must drive us to proclaim the word of the cross.

By proclamation I do not just mean preaching in the sense of sermons. I simply mean sharing the message of the gospel with people. The word *preaching* in the New Testament is a declaration of the gospel to unbelievers. It takes many different forms, including dialogue and conversation. It is not the exclusive preserve of a preacher in a pulpit. In fact, it is much more likely to take place over a cup of tea or when reading the Bible with an unbeliever. But whatever form it takes, making known the message of the gospel must be central.

Again, this is a truth that runs throughout the Bible. God rules through his Word and he reestablishes his rule through his Word. But let us focus on Luke's Gospel. Luke has a lot to say about the poor. He speaks of a future time of reversal when the first shall be last, and the last shall be first. Luke demonstrates the certainty of this word about the future to Theophilus by showing how this reversal has been prefigured in the ministry of Jesus (Luke 1:4). Jesus welcomed the marginalized while condemning the powerful. So Luke calls on his readers to associate with the poor, persecuted Christian community even though this may mean forsaking their social privileges. In all this, God's Word is central. This is how hope for the future is conveyed. And God's Word is sufficient to sustain believers in this world.

Luke 8:4–21

In the parable of the sower the kingdom is advanced as the seed is scattered. Jesus says the seed is *"the word of God"* (v. 11), and the good soil consists of those "who, hearing the word, hold it fast in an honest and good heart, and bear fruit with patience" (v. 15). So the true family of Jesus is defined as "those who hear the word of God and do it" (v. 21).

Luke 10:38–42

There is an echo here in Luke 10:38–42 of the parable of the sower. Martha's problem is that she is "anxious and troubled about many things" (v. 41). The word *"anxious"* is the same word as *"cares"* in the description of rocky soil in the parable of the sower (8:14). These cares divert people from the Word of God, and so it is with Martha. In contrast Mary chooses "the good portion" (10:42), which is to listen to Jesus's words.

Luke 11:27–32

A woman says to Jesus that blessed is the womb that bore him. "But he said, 'Blessed rather are those who hear the word of God and keep it!'" (v. 28). He then responds to the request of those who were demanding that he perform a sign (11:16). The only sign that will be given is the sign of Jonah. In Matthew's account it is a reference to the resurrection. But in Luke the focus is on Jonah the preacher. They want a sign, but all they get is a preacher. The word of God is enough. The Queen of the South who came to hear the words of Solomon and the people of Nineveh who responded to the word preached by Jonah will condemn those who now reject that word (11:45–52).

Luke 16:19–31

In Luke 16 Jesus tells the story of a beggar called Lazarus who lives at the gate of a rich man. When both Lazarus and the rich man die, Lazarus goes to heaven with Abraham while the rich man goes to hell. The rich man wants Abraham to send Lazarus with water to cool his pain. When he is refused, he makes a second request. He asks Lazarus to be sent to his brothers to warn of God's judgment. Abraham replies: "If they do not hear Moses and the Prophets, neither will they be convinced if someone should rise from the dead" (v. 31). In other words, God's Word is enough. God's Word is all we need. Nothing else will persuade us if God's Word does not persuade us—not even apparitions of the dead.

Luke 24:25–27, 44–47

What does the risen Christ do on the first Easter day? He teaches the Scriptures. If anyone could simply have declared the truth and elicited faith, it must surely have been the Lord Jesus freshly

risen from the grave. But he spends that first Easter day conduct-
ing a Bible study. He brings comfort and faith to his disciples by
opening the Scriptures for them. Here is someone risen from the
dead—just as the rich man had requested (16:30)—but what he
does is proclaim the Word of God.

So the proclamation of the gospel must be central to Christian
social involvement. The form our gospel proclamation takes will
vary depending on the context. In situations of extreme persecution it may be no more than an ongoing Christian presence. A
commitment to reconciling people to God through the proclamation of the gospel should not be taken as a justification for
bad evangelism. Often in such debates, people highlight the worst
cases of evangelism as if a commitment to the centrality of proclamation forced you to justify such activities. A commitment to
gospel proclamation does not mean a commitment to bad, un-
contextualized, manipulative, or crass gospel proclamation. But
in social involvement there will always be a commitment to the
reconciliation of the poor with God through the gospel. The proclamation of the gospel must be at the heart of Christian social
involvement. Our aim will always be that the poor are blessed in
this life *and* for all eternity.

Summary

We have seen the priority in the Bible of the eternal future. This
means that the greatest need of the poor is to be reconciled with
God through Jesus Christ. This takes place through the Holy
Spirit as people respond to the Word of God. The proclamation
of the gospel must therefore be central to Christian work among
the poor.

Let us return to the characters we met in the introduction. We
have seen that Catherine has a good case. The Bible does compel us
to show concern for the poor and seek justice in society. It gives
us a mandate for cultural and social involvement. But we have
seen, too, that Douglas has proper concerns. We must be commit-

ted to the reconciliation of the poor to God through the gospel. This means that proclaiming the gospel must be at the heart of all that we do as Christians and as churches. In the next chapter we will consider the relationship between social involvement and gospel proclamation, bringing the positions of Catherine and Douglas together.

4

Social Involvement and Proclamation

The Lausanne Congress in 1974 marked a key turning point in the rediscovery by evangelicals of the social involvement that had been so much part of their heritage until the twentieth century, as we saw in chapter 2. But not all were happy. Arthur Johnston, professor of mission at Trinity Evangelical Divinity School, Illinois, initially welcomed Lausanne. But shortly after, he wrote *The Battle for World Evangelism* (1978) in which he questioned the position taken in the Lausanne Covenant. He decried Lausanne's "holistic" view of mission. Johnston did not oppose social action *per se* but saw mission as evangelism and evangelism alone. He feared that if sociopolitical involvement was included as part of mission, then evangelism would inevitably be edged out. Johnston accused John Stott of having "dethroned evangelism as *the* only historical aim of mission."[1] In an open letter in response to Johnston, published in *Christianity Today*, Stott argued that the words and works of Jesus "belonged indissolubly to one another." He said that rather than dethroning evangelism, he had sought to "enthrone love as the essential historical motivation for mission."[2]

---

[1] Arthur P. Johnston, *The Battle for World Evangelism* (Carol Stream, IL: Tyndale, 1978), 302–3.
[2] John Stott, "The Battle for World Evangelism: An Open Response to Arthur Johnston," *Christianity Today* (January 4, 1979).

Social Action Can Follow,
Precede, and Accompany Evangelism

John Stott also wrote privately to Arthur Johnston proposing they meet to talk. He also suggested that the Lausanne Committee for World Evangelization convene a conference on the issue. The Consultation on the Relationship between Evangelism and Social Responsibility met in June 1982 at Grand Rapids, Michigan. Both Stott and Johnston had served on the organizing committee, and the committee had gone to great lengths to involve people from different perspectives within evangelicalism. This made for a stormy meeting. The papers circulated beforehand were sharply critical of one another. John Stott confessed to being "almost in despair."[3] As the consultation progressed, however, the participants began to understand one another's concerns and by the grace of God came to a good measure of agreement.

The report of the Grand Rapids consultation, *Evangelism and Social Responsibility: An Evangelical Commitment*, remains a significant statement on the subject. It explains the relationship between evangelism and social responsibility in three ways:

1) Social Activity Is the Consequence of Evangelism

Social activity is one of the aims of evangelism since people are saved for the good works that God has prepared for them (Eph. 2:10). Repentant people become socially responsible people. Dr. Kiran Martin was converted from Hinduism as a teenager. Her involvement in the lives of the slum dwellers of New Delhi stemmed directly from that moment. And her experience has been repeated thousands of times.

Moreover, people bring their problems with them when they come into God's kingdom. Churches planted among the poor will be churches facing issues of poverty and injustice. So church planting leads to social involvement. In the area of Iringa in Tan-

---

[3] Cited in Tim Chester, *Awakening to a World of Need: The Recovery of Evangelical Social Concern* (Nottingham, UK: Inter-Varsity, 1993), 122.

zania, the Anglican church is growing rapidly, the result of an enthusiastic commitment to mission. Bishop Mdimi Mhogolo helped establish a new diocese in the area, now led by a dynamic evangelist. But conversion is just the beginning. "God has accepted these people in the kingdom, so they look to God and the church to answer their prayers," Bishop Mhogolo told the evangelical development agency, Tearfund. "They ask what he is doing for health, education, food and so on. The church is automatically involved in development." The evangelistic ministry of the church is backed by education, health, and agricultural development programs— a model repeated across the Anglican church of Tanzania. "So much material in the Bible brings out that God is involved in all we do," said Bishop Mhogolo, "transforming our lives spiritually and physically."[4]

2) Social Activity Can Be a Bridge to Evangelism

Social action can break down prejudice and create openings for the gospel. The love shown through social involvement can create opportunities for the gospel that would not otherwise have existed. (Although, as the report warns, social provision should not be used as a bribe to create "rice Christians"—people who are "Christians" only in order to gain inducements.)

Stephen Rand, Tearfund's prayer and campaign director, describes visiting Ethiopia shortly after the famine of 1984. There he met Daniel, a church leader with a vision of transformation. The Kale Heywit Church had persuaded the government to give them a barren area of land, and Daniel hoped to work with the local people to reforest it. Three years later Rand again met Daniel. The 6-inch seedlings he had been shown were now 30 feet tall, and the land was productive once again. The Marxist government was so impressed that it had given the church another plot of land. But, explains Rand, Daniel went on to explain there had been another dimension of the transformation process:

[4] *Evangelism and Social Responsibility: An Evangelical Commitment*, Lausanne Occasional Paper 21, 1982, http://www.lausanne.org/en/documents/lops/79-lop-21.html.

The land was situated in a largely Muslim area of the country. Missionaries had preached for twenty years or so without noticeable effect. But now the local people were puzzled that the church had come to work there, providing them with food in exchange for their labour, and creating an oasis of fruitfulness where there had previously been only desert. It had made them ask the question why. And Daniel had been only too ready to tell them that it was because of God's love for them, a love that could not only see the landscape transformed, but a love that could transform their lives as well. As a result, some had made a commitment to Christ, and a church had been established. Planting trees had been persuasive preaching.[5]

3) Social Activity Is the Partner of Evangelism

Evangelism and social action have often been partners in a mutually reinforcing way. Evangelism strengthens social action as the gospel changes people's attitudes and worldview. Social action can gain hearing for the gospel message. The report described this partnership in terms of a marriage or like two wings of a bird.

Florence Veboah is the founder of GHACOE (Ghana Congress on Evangelism)—a ministry to women based in Accra, the capital of Ghana. She wanted to see the kind of Christianity "that exhibits transformed character . . . that enjoys the power of God that would give fulfilment to women, whether single or married." Her solution was to pass on practical skills to give women self-worth and a new start as well as to address their spiritual needs. "Our ministry is holistic," she says; "we try to meet the total need of the total person." Mary's experience is typical. "Before the project started I had no work and little money," she explains. "I felt frustrated and depressed and turned to drink. Now I'm able to earn money. I can feed the family. I have stopped drinking and turned to the Lord." "The very demeanour of our women changes when they are filled with the Holy Spirit," says Florence. "They become beautiful inside. They are helped to see that life is meaningful and they are

---

[5]Stephen Rand, "Love Your Neighbour As Yourself," in *The Care of Creation*, ed. R. J. Berry (Nottingham, UK: Inter-Varsity, 2000), 146.

precious to Jesus. The joy of feeling accepted by God makes them confident in life and happy women."

Social action, then, can precede, accompany, and follow evangelism.

Given this relationship, evangelism, according to the Grand Rapids Report, has priority only in two senses. First, it has a logical priority, since Christian social responsibility presupposes socially responsible Christians, though this does not mean evangelism must come first in every context. Second, evangelism has a priority that stems from the unique nature of the gospel, for it "relates to people's eternal destiny, and in bringing them Good News of salvation Christians are doing what nobody else can do."[6] The report went on to acknowledge that in reality the choice is largely conceptual. In practice, the ministry of Jesus, in which the two were inseparable, is to be our model. Indeed, the report goes further, saying that "evangelism and social responsibility, while distinct from one another, are integrally related in our proclamation of and obedience to the gospel."[7] It says evangelism and service are both forms of witness to Christ.

Integral Mission

This idea of an integral relationship was affirmed more recently when evangelical development agencies from around the world met in 2001 in Oxford to form the "Micah Network." They produced a statement called "The Micah Declaration on Integral Mission." The term "integral mission" comes from the Spanish "misión integral," the term commonly used in Latin America for what others describe as "holistic ministry," "Christian development," or "transformation." Each of these terms has its merits and its weaknesses. "Holistic" was used to indicate a concern for the whole person, but in recent years it has become widely used with quite different connotations (holistic medicine and so on), which makes its continued use potentially confusing. Because of the dominance of economics in many people's thinking, "development" runs the

---

[6] *Evangelism and Social Responsibility.*
[7] Ibid., 24.

risk of implying that wealthy countries are more developed and therefore superior to poorer countries. The problem with the term "transformation" is that it can mean anything and therefore means nothing. It allows people to undertake activities in the name of mission that exclude social involvement or, more commonly, that exclude proclamation. Each of these terms contributes something, but none quite does the job on its own. The Micah Declaration uses them all, but "integral mission" was adopted as the central term. The declaration defines it as follows:

> Integral mission or holistic transformation is the proclamation and demonstration of the gospel. It is not simply that evangelism and social involvement are to be done alongside each other. Rather, in integral mission our proclamation has social consequences as we call people to love and repentance in all areas of life. And our social involvement has evangelistic consequences as we bear witness to the transforming grace of Jesus Christ. If we ignore the world we betray the word of God which sends us out to serve the world. If we ignore the word of God we have nothing to bring to the world.[8]

To bring the relationship between evangelism and social action into sharp focus I want to make three assertions: (1) evangelism and social action are distinct activities; (2) proclamation is central; and (3) evangelism and social action are inseparable.

1) Evangelism and Social Action Are Distinct Activities

Some refuse to make any distinction between evangelism and social action. They conflate social action and proclamation into one activity. The problem is that this usually ends up with one aspect—and it is usually evangelism—being lost. This approach, says Melba Maggay, "tends to lose sight of the proclamation aspect of the gospel, the fact that it is news, a thing you shout from the housetops."[9] So it is important to retain the idea that proclama-

---

[8] "The Micah Declaration on Integral Mission," in *Justice, Mercy and Humility: Integral Mission and the Poor*, ed. Tim Chester (Carlisle, UK: Paternoster, 2002), 19.
[9] Melba Maggay, *Transforming Society* (Oxford: Regnum, 1994), 17.

tion and social involvement are distinct activities. Attempts to fuse development and proclamation cannot work from a biblical perspective for two reasons.

First, social involvement is about effecting change in history. It is historically provisional. It can be undone. Proclamation, on the other hand, is about effecting eternal change. I remember consoling a friend after the Rwandan massacres in 1994. He had spent four years involved in community development in Rwanda. Now it seemed his years of hard work had been overturned in a matter of days. The fruit of social action can be undone; the fruit of proclamation cannot.

Second, social involvement at its best is about harnessing the resources within a community. It is about empowering a community through their participation. The alternative is a paternalistic approach that is short-term, creating dependency in its beneficiaries. In good development an understanding of the problem and its solutions comes to some extent from within a community. In contrast, the message of the gospel is that we are powerless and cannot participate in our salvation. Both an understanding of the problem and the solution must come from outside the community. This outside message does not come from Western technology, money, or expertise. It comes from heaven. This is one reason for the emphasis in John's Gospel that Jesus is "from heaven" (John 3:13, 31; 6:33, 38, 42, 50, 51, 58).

2) Proclamation Is Central

Many evangelicals want to argue that evangelism and social action are equal activities. They describe evangelism and social action as two wings of a bird or the blades of a pair of scissors. While evangelism and social action are partners in many situations, it is inadequate to think of them as corresponding activities of equal impact. As we have seen, the greatest need of the poor, as it is for all people, is to be reconciled with God and escape his wrath. Only the message of the gospel can do this. The adage, often attributed to

Saint Francis of Assisi, that "we should preach always, sometimes using words," will not do. Social action can demonstrate the gospel, but without the communication of the gospel message, social action is like a signpost pointing nowhere. Indeed, without the message of the gospel, it points in the wrong direction. If all we do are good works among people, then we point to ourselves and our charitable acts. People will think well of us, but not of Jesus Christ. We may even convey the message that salvation is achieved by good works. Or we may convey the message that what matters most is economic and social betterment. We must not do social action without evangelism.

3) Evangelism and Social Action Are Inseparable

Given that the greatest need of people is to be reconciled with God, and given that this need can be met only through the message of the gospel, it might seem logical to say that evangelism has priority. It might seem a short step from saying that proclamation is central to saying that evangelism is our priority. The problem is that it is not clear what "priority" means in this context. It suggests a choice in which evangelism should be chosen or competing priorities in which social action can be neglected. We prioritize by making a list and doing the activities at the top of the list. If there is no time left for items lower down the list, then this does not matter because we have deemed such things less important. The implication of saying evangelism has priority in this sense is that it does not matter if we have no time for social action.

But such choices rarely bear any relationship to reality. In our involvement in the lives of others, we cannot choose to ignore their social needs. We cannot treat people in isolation from their context. Evangelism alone might make sense in the lecture room. It may even just about make sense in a wealthy suburb. But it makes no sense at all when working among the poor. Mission takes place in and through relationships, and relationships are multifaceted. Proclamation should be central, but a center implies a context, and our proclamation should take place in the context of a life of love.

Some people say that church leaders should focus on teaching the Word of God. They are right. Those who have been given the gift of Bible teaching by God should teach God's Word. The problem comes when this is combined with an unevangelical clericalism in which the role of the pastor-teacher defines the identity of the whole church. Church life revolves around the leader, so such ministry is seen as the only valid ministry. But this is not a New Testament view of the church. In the church each member has distinctive gifts from God and therefore a distinctive ministry to fulfill. Paul uses the image of a body to highlight the way that no member should feel inferior (1 Cor. 12:15–20). But neither should any member feel superior, despising the gifts of others (1 Cor. 12:21–24). Peter draws a distinction between gifts of the Word and gifts of service (1 Pet. 4:10–11). In the Reformed and Puritan traditions, from which much evangelicalism sprung, the role of the deacons was to be responsible for the social involvement of the church, following the pattern of Acts 6:1–7 (though John Owen stressed that pastors retained overall responsibility for the care of the poor).[10] Only more recently have deacons commonly become those who manage church property.

Social action and evangelism should be neither identified with one another nor separated. Evangelism and social action should be viewed as *distinct but inseparable* activities in our mission to the poor in which *proclamation is central*. In any relationship with the poor or with a poor community we must as evangelicals be looking for opportunities to share the message of the gospel. This is not because our social action is invalid without evangelism. It is because love requires that we share the message of hope that meets people's greatest need.

The relationship between evangelism and social action can be thought of as the relationship between text and context. The first

---

[10] See John Calvin, *Institutes*, 4.3.9 and 4.4.5; and John Owen, *True Nature of a Gospel Church*, vol. 16, *The Works of John Owen* (Edinburgh: Banner of Truth, 1968), 143–51.

rule for reading the Bible is to look at the context. If you want to understand a *text* (a word, a phrase, a paragraph, or a story) you need to understand it in the light of its wider *context*. In fact, that is true of all texts. Consider the following statement: "I'm mad about my car." The word "mad" could mean enthusiastic and excited or it could mean angry and annoyed. Taken on its own, the statement is unclear. But add a bit of context and it becomes clearer: "I'm mad about my car; it was stolen from right outside my house." Context clarifies a text. It can even alter what we originally thought it meant. Texts truly make sense only in a context.

The same is true of the gospel message. The "text" of the gospel message is heard by people in a context. It is not a question of whether it should be. It always is. Whenever you share the gospel with people, they will understand it within a certain context. Our text—the message we proclaim—will be interpreted by the context of our lives and our life together as Christian communities. Proclamation cannot take place apart from a context. The question is whether that context matches the message of the transforming grace of Jesus Christ.

If you talk about God's grace while constantly being legalistic about other people's lifestyles, then you should not be surprised if you are misunderstood. People will think the gospel is about adherence to rules and norms. Nor will you be understood if you talk about God's love while you exhibit bitterness and envy. Jesus does not simply tell Zacchaeus that God graciously accepts the lost (Luke 19:1–10). He embodies that message in his request to eat with Zacchaeus. He expresses the inclusion of God's grace by sharing a table with Zacchaeus. His actions reinforce and embody his message that "the Son of Man came to seek and to save the lost" (Luke 19:10).

Peter says in his first letter: "But in your hearts honor Christ the Lord as holy, always being prepared to make a defense to anyone who asks you for a reason for the hope that is in you; yet do it with gentleness and respect" (1 Pet. 3:15). Commenting on this, Jim Wallis says:

Evangelism in our day has largely become a packaged production, a mass-marketed experience in which evangelists strain to
answer that question which nobody is asking. Modern evangelists
must go through endless contortions to convince people that they
are missing something that Christians have. Without the visible
witness of a distinct style of life, evangelists must become aggres-
sive and gimmicky, their methods reduced to salesmanship and
showmanship. Evangelism often becomes a special activity awk-
wardly conducted . . . instead of being a simple testimony rising
out of a community whose life together invites questions from
the surrounding society. When the life of the church no longer
raises any questions, evangelism degenerates.[11]

When the context of our lives does not match the text of our
message, we should not be surprised if evangelism becomes hard
work. In contrast, I want to suggest there are two contexts that
best enable people to understand the message of the gospel: loving
actions and loving community.

1) Loving Actions

The context that properly interprets the gospel message is love. In
our love for the "other"—especially the marginalized—we model
the grace of God. We all recognize this at an individual level. Even
those who deny the place of Christian social action still want
Christians to live godly lives. They do not suppose that godly living
is a distraction from the task of proclaiming the gospel. Quite the
opposite. Godly lives commend the gospel. Paul tells Titus how he
is to teach slaves to live "so that in everything they may adorn the
doctrine of God our Savior" (Titus 2:10). In the same way the good
works of social action commend the gospel. Peter says: "Keep your
conduct among the Gentiles honorable, so that when they speak
against you as evildoers, they may see your good deeds and glorify
God on the day of visitiation" (1 Pet. 2:12). Part of the problem is
that we read the Bible with our Western individualistic glasses on.

---

[11]Jim Wallis, *A Call to Conversion* (Oxford, UK: Lion, 1981), 19–20, 29.

It is not just my private life that adorns the gospel; it is also my public life. It is not just what individual Christians do, but how the Christian community lives.

2) Loving Community

Jesus said: "A new commandment I give to you, that you love one another: just as I have loved you, you also are to love one another. By this all people will know that you are my disciples, if you have love for one another" (John 13:34). How will people see the gospel at work in this world? How will people know that Jesus is from God (John 17:23)? Through the life of the Christian community. Lesslie Newbigin describes the congregation as "the hermeneutic of the gospel."[12] In my experience, people are often attracted to the Christian community before they are attracted to the Christian message. This means we must ensure unbelievers experience the church as a caring, inclusive community. And that does not just mean a warm handshake at the door; it means drawing people into the network of relationships that make up the church. It means ensuring that your unbelieving friends meet your Christian friends so they can observe how you relate to one another. The church must be a community of gospel people, not something you attend on Sunday.

As Christians we are witnesses to Christ, whether we like it or not. It is not a question of whether we should be witnesses. The question is what kind of witnesses we are. Do we help people understand the gospel? Think about the contexts in which you are already a witness. Then think about how you can build on the links and interests you already have. You do not have to start a big church project. You could simply join an existing voluntary organization. You could simply be more intentional about something you are already doing. Think through:

- How can I be more intentional about sharing the gospel?
- What can I do to show love to people?

[12] Lesslie Newbigin, *The Gospel in a Pluralist Society* (London: SPCK, 1989), 222–33.

- Are there Christians with similar interests or contacts with whom I could work?
- Are there things I can do to take the gospel outside Christian circles?
- How can I introduce people to my network of Christian relationships?

Reminding them of his ministry among them, Paul writes to the Thessalonians: "So, being affectionately desirous of you, we were ready to share with you not only the gospel of God but also our own selves, because you had become very dear to us" (1 Thess. 2:8). Paul shared both the gospel and his life with people—Word and life together. Yet often we divide into those who share the gospel without sharing our lives and those who share our lives without sharing the gospel. Some engage in cold evangelism outside the context of a relationship. Others form deep relationships with people but never have the courage to challenge them with the claims of the gospel.

Thirty years ago the theological struggle for integral mission was to gain acceptance for the place of social involvement in mission. In some quarters this is still an area of debate. Yet at the same time, among a new generation of evangelicals it is the necessity of making evangelism integral that needs to be affirmed. Brought up in a postmodern culture that sees a commitment to absolute truth as arrogant, this generation hesitates to proclaim the revealed Word of God. Many Christians today—particularly in the West—readily assent to social action but are less sure about proclaiming the liberating truth of the gospel. But a commitment to integral mission is as much a commitment to make evangelism integral with social action as it is to make social action integral with evangelism.

Our evangelism should have social consequences as we call people to follow Christ in every area of life, reflecting the justice and love of God in obedience to his will and doing the good works that God purposes for them. Our social action should have evangelistic consequences as we demonstrate the love of God and the power of the gospel and as we build relationships with people that provide opportunities to tell them of the good news.

Summary

In describing the relationship between evangelism and social action, we have seen that:

- evangelism and social action are distinct activities;
- proclamation is central;
- evangelism and social action are inseparable, especially in ministry among the poor.

The "text" of our gospel proclamation is best understood in the context of loving actions and loving community.

In chapters 1 and 2 we looked at the case for Christian social involvement. In chapter 3 we saw the importance of proclaiming the gospel to the poor. In this chapter we have seen how social involvement and gospel proclamation belong together. The next three chapters explore the relationship between the content of the gospel and social involvement. Chapter 5 questions whether advances in social justice should be seen as salvation and the coming of God's kingdom. Chapters 6 and 7 explore how the gospel message is specifically good news for the poor and for the rich.

5

Social Involvement and the Kingdom of God

Suppose a well is dug in a village bringing clean water for the first time or a drug addict is rehabilitated in the context of a loving community. Is this an advance of the kingdom of God? Is it an act of divine salvation? Does it make a difference if the drilling team or the drug addict's community are Christians? Or suppose an oppressive regime is toppled or a piece of legislation is passed that improves the lot of the poor. Can we say that God's kingdom has come in some way?

Is Social Justice Salvation?

Is social justice salvation? Some evangelicals have argued that it is. They maintain that salvation exists beyond the church and that the kingdom of God can come even when Christ has not been confessed as Lord. For example:

> All the earth is the Lord's and so we trace the Spirit at work beyond the Church, especially in movements that make for human dignity and liberation.[1]

> Not infrequently, if we have eyes to see this, God is advancing his kingdom through those who may not recognize this but whose

---

[1] Nigel Wright, *The Radical Evangelical* (London: SPCK, 1996), 112.

quest for justice and wholeness, for liberty and community, is contributing towards the kingdom's advance.[2]

Where we see barriers broken down, can we divorce this from God's will seen in Christ's victory over the powers on the cross. . . . This gives us a basis for seeing God at work in society beyond the church applying the effects of Christ's victory on the cross through social change.[3]

The kingdom comes wherever Jesus overcomes the Evil One. This happens (or ought to happen) in fullest measure in the church. But it also happens in society.[4]

[The kingdom is seen, not only in the church,] but also in God's kingdom activity in the world beyond the church . . . as the just relationships that belong to the kingdom are established in society.[5]

This identification of social justice in history with salvation or kingdom distinguishes its advocates from the evangelical social activists of the nineteenth century. It has more in common with the "social gospel," a movement associated with Walter Rauschenbusch, a pastor and professor in New York and author of *Christianity and the Social Order* (1907) and *A Theology for the Social Gospel* (1917). Rauschenbusch saw the kingdom of God as the construction of a Christian society in history. He contrasted what he thought of as the old gospel of the saved soul with the new gospel of the kingdom of God. In the early twentieth century many evangelicals reacted against the social gospel by rejecting all social involvement. Even today some evangelicals dismiss any evangelical social involvement as a return to the social gospel. But evangelical social involvement is not a return to the social gospel but back beyond

---

[2] Stuart Murray, *Church Planting: Laying Foundations* (Carlisle, UK: Paternoster, 1998), 43.

[3] Cited in Melvin Tinker, *Evangelical Concerns: Rediscovering the Christian Mind in Issues Facing the Church Today* (Fearn, Ross-shire, UK: Mentor, 2001), 152.

[4] David Bosch, *Witness to the World: The Christian Mission in Theological Perspective* (London: Marshall, Morgan & Scott, 1980), 209.

[5] Vinay Samuel and Chris Sugden, "Toward a Theology of Social Change," in *Evangelicals and Development*, ed. Ronald J. Sider (Carlisle, UK: Paternoster, 1981), 52.

that to the evangelicalism of the Great Awakening, the Reformation, and biblical Christianity. The problem is that what is advocated by some does share some features of the social gospel, even if they also continue to affirm the importance of evangelism. The kingdom of God is identified with social advances within history.

But if we are to be true to the Bible, we must maintain that salvation does *not* exist in history beyond the church and that in the New Testament the kingdom of God comes *only* as Christ is acknowledged as king. We have seen that Jesus is Lord of all of life, but we have also seen that his lordship is rejected in this world. In the next chapter we will see that salvation includes social liberation, but we will also see that this liberation is a future reality that is anticipated only in and through the Christian community.

The Greek word for *kingdom* refers both to "rule" and to the "realm" in which that rule is exercised. Those who want to use the salvation language of social justice emphasize the kingdom as an activity. They often talk of *kingdom* in quite general terms as God's activity in history. But Jesus uses *kingdom* in both senses, as an activity and as a realm. He often talks in terms of entering the kingdom of God, and you cannot "enter" an activity. In its fullest sense the kingdom of God refers to the future rule of God over a new humanity in a new creation. But when people respond to the gospel and submit to the rule of God, they enter the kingdom in the present—and, moreover, they also experience a foretaste of the blessings of his future reign ahead of time through the Holy Spirit.

The real problem with equating social justice with salvation is that it separates the kingdom of God from the gospel. It is not enough to say, as some people do, that the gospel is big enough to include social justice in history outside the confession of Christ as Lord. The gospel is good *news—a message, a word* that must be proclaimed. The kingdom of God comes as God's Word is proclaimed and people submit to the kingship of Jesus. From creation onwards God has ruled through his Word. And today he continues to rule through the word of the gospel. Through the gospel we call on people to submit to the rule of God and his Messiah. As the Great

Commission makes clear, the rule of Christ is exercised through the gospel.

> Jesus came and said to them, "All authority in heaven and on earth has been given to me. Go therefore and make disciples of all nations, baptizing them in the name of the Father and of the Son and of the Holy Spirit, teaching them to observe all that I have commanded you. And behold, I am with you always, to the end of the age." (Matt. 28:18–20)

All authority has been given to Christ, so he sends us into the world to call the nations to obedience. It is through the preaching of the gospel that Jesus is wielding his scepter in the world. Through the gospel we command people to submit to Jesus. Through the gospel judgment is passed on people who continue to reject him. We are ambassadors bringing a pronouncement from the coming king. We are like heralds going to the citizens of a country to announce that a king is coming who rightly claims their allegiance. Those who currently rule them are tyrants and usurpers. If they acknowledge his lordship over them, they will experience his rule as blessing, life, and salvation. If they reject him, they will experience him as their conqueror and judge. We must deliver this message graciously and gently; we cannot manipulate or force anyone to repent (1 Pet. 3:16). But one day all people will bow the knee before Jesus and confess him as Lord (Phil. 2:9–11).[6]

In Mark's Gospel Jesus begins his ministry by announcing the coming of God's kingdom and calling upon people to repent (1:14–15). Mark shows us the authority of Jesus over people (1:16–20), in teaching (1:22), over evil spirits (1:23–27), and over sickness (1:29–34). Jesus even claims authority to forgive sins (2:1–12). He exercises authority over the natural world (4:35–41) and over death (5:21–24, 35–43). But in Mark 2 and 3 we get a different series of stories. We get a sequence that describes the opposition and rejection that Jesus faces. The teaching of chapter 4 takes place "on

---

[6] See Tim Chester, *From Creation to New Creation: Understanding the Bible Story*, 2nd ed. (London: The Good Book Company, 2010), 93–131.

another occasion" (v. 1). In other words, it is linked by the theme of the kingdom of God rather than chronologically with what precedes it. The teaching of chapter 4 explains the events of chapters 2 and 3. The stories of chapters 2 and 3 are stories of rejection. The Jews expected the Messiah to come in power and glory. So if the message of Jesus is rejected, how can it be right when he proclaims the coming of God's kingdom?

1) The Kingdom Comes Secretly

The answer is that the kingdom comes secretly. The Jews expected the kingdom would come in triumph. God would sweep away his enemies in a blaze of glory and power. But the secret of the kingdom is that even though this has not happened, the kingdom has come. The coming of the kingdom is a secret given only to some (Mark 4:11). It has come in a hidden way. In Mark 4:30–31 Jesus likens the kingdom of God to a mustard seed. A mustard seed was proverbially small. In the same way, the kingdom of God appears small and insignificant. Nor is it simply the case that the kingdom comes secretly; it is actually opposed. And that is the exact opposite of what we expect. We expect the kingdom of God to come in glory and triumph, but here the kingdom is despised and rejected. In a sense, though it is hidden, it is revealed in persecution, opposition, and rejection. It is seen in an opposite form: rejection.

2) The Kingdom Comes Graciously

Mark begins his Gospel with a quote from Malachi. It speaks of a forerunner who will prepare the way for the coming of God. This is what it says in context:

> Behold, I send my messenger, and he will prepare the way before me. And the Lord whom you seek will suddenly come to his temple; and the messenger of the covenant in whom you delight, behold, he is coming, says the Lord of hosts. But who can endure the day of his coming, and who can stand when he appears? For he is like a refiner's fire and like fullers' soap. (Mal. 3:1–2)

The people complain: "Where is the God of justice?" (Mal. 2:17). But Malachi says: God is coming, but when he comes who can endure his coming? When the God of justice comes in triumph and judgment he will come down your street. He will judge you. And who can stand? This is the dilemma of God's people: we long for God to intervene in justice and establish his rule. But his coming will be *our* defeat and *our* judgment. God's solution is that the coming of God's kingdom takes place in two stages. He comes first secretly and graciously. There is judgment, but the king is the one who is judged. Judgment takes place at the cross, and it falls on the king. He dies in our place. The kingdom comes first in grace.

John the Baptist announced that "even now the axe is laid to the root of the trees. Every tree therefore that does not bear good fruit is cut down and thrown into the fire" (Matt. 3:10). But when Jesus comes, the axe does not fall. John is not vindicated but imprisoned. So John the Baptist sends messengers to Jesus to ask if he is truly the Christ. Jesus responds by saying: "Go and tell John what you hear and see: the blind recive their sight and the lame walk, lepers are cleansed and the deaf hear, and the dead are raised up, and the poor have good news preached to them. And blessed is the one who is not offended by me" (Matt. 11:4–6). Jesus's response is an allusion to Isaiah 35:4–6 and 61:1–2. Jesus is portraying himself as the fulfillment of the messianic promises. His miracles demonstrate that he is the one who brings God's promised future. But Jesus has edited his sources. Both passages in Isaiah speak of judgment, but Jesus does not mention that God "will come with vengeance, with the recompense of God" (Isa. 35:4), or "the day of vengeance of our God" (Isa. 61:2). The kingdom has come, but the not the day of vengeance—not yet. John the Baptist had said that when Christ comes, "his winnowing fork is in his hand, and he will clear his threshing floor and gather his wheat into the barn, but the chaff he will burn with unquenchable fire" (Matt. 3:11–12). But first the kingdom comes graciously.

3) The Kingdom Comes through God's Word

As Jesus is opposed by the leaders of Israel and his own family (Mark 3:20–21), he chooses the Twelve to form a new Israel (matching the twelve tribes of Israel). And in 3:31–35 Jesus calls into being a new family—the new family of God. In the midst of this opposition and rejection, a new community is born. The kingdom comes through a new community, a new people, a new family. But notice that what forms this new community and what marks them out is the word of Jesus—the gospel: "Whoever does the will of God, he is my brother and sister and mother" (Mark 3:35). The sower in the parable of the sower sows the word (4:14). How does the kingdom come? Through the Word of God. How is the kingdom advanced? Through the sowing of God's Word. The growth of the kingdom comes when people "hear the word" of God and "accept it" (4:20). The new family is built around those who do God's will. The new Israel is constituted by the preaching of the gospel (3:14). The kingdom grows when people hear and accept the Word of God. Think of Mark's readers. Jesus is gone, ascended into heaven. How is the king present? Mark's response is: through his Word.

4) The Kingdom Will Come in Glory

So far we have seen that the kingdom of God comes secretly. It is hidden. The Jews expected the kingdom to come in glory. But in Jesus it comes in a hidden way, a persecuted way. The Jews expected the kingdom to come in power and judgment. But in Jesus it comes in a gracious way through the gospel. It comes as the gift of salvation and the call to repentance. But the Jews were not wrong in their expectations. The kingdom *will* come in glory and power and judgment. We should not think the secret, gracious presence of the kingdom means the kingdom will not come in triumph. Despite the ordinariness of life, the "harvest has come" (Mark 4:26–29). Once the seed is sown, the harvest will come. Life goes on. Day follows night. We sleep, we get up, we get tired and go to bed again. Life just seems to go round and round. But all the time we can be sure of this: God's kingdom is coming. And *the harvest will be great* (4:30–32). Despite its small beginnings, the harvest will be great. The kingdom may be secret. It may be hidden. It may be opposed. But make no mistake: it will come in glory. It will fill the earth. It will offer refuge to people throughout the world. It will triumph. The kingdom is secret and concealed, but one day it will be revealed and disclosed (4:21–22). One day it will come in glory and power. So, says Jesus, get ready by hearing and accepting the word—the gospel of the kingdom (4:23–25).

So the kingdom of God cannot be separated from the gospel. The Spirit mediates the coming reign of God through the gospel so that Christ rules now by his word of promise. So, as the Lausanne Covenant says, political liberation is not salvation.[7] And the Grand Rapids report speaks of salvation as "new life . . . new community . . . new world," but the new community is the church, and the new world is spoken of only in future terms.[8] Although the report acknowledges that some found the use of salvation language appropriate for the emergence of justice and peace in the wider community, it continues, "Most of us, however, consider that [it] is more prudent and biblical to reserve the vocabulary of salvation for the experience of reconciliation with God through Christ and its direct consequences."[9] John Stott insists that "the kingdom of God in the New Testament is a fundamentally *christological* concept, and that as such it may be said to exist only where Jesus Christ is consciously acknowledged as Lord," although "the righteous standards of the kingdom . . . may to some extent spill over into the world as a result of Christian influence."[10]

In his contribution to the Grand Rapids consultation Ron Sider

---

[7] The Lausanne Covenant, "Paragraph 5: Christian Social Responsibility," *Making Christ Known: Historic Mission Documents from the Lausanne Movement 1974–1989*, ed. John Stott (Carlisle, UK: Paternoster, 1996), 24.
[8] *Evangelism and Social Responsibility: An Evangelical Commitment*, Lausanne Occasional Paper 21, 1982, http://www.lausanne.org/en/documents/lops/79-lop-21.html.
[9] Ibid.
[10] Ronald J. Sider and John Stott, *Evangelism, Salvation and Social Justice* (Nottingham, UK: Grove Books, 1977), 23.

says: "It is important to note that *absolutely none* of the scores of New Testament texts on the kingdom of God speak of the presence of the kingdom apart from the conscious confession of Christ. . . . There seems no warrant in the New Testament for talking about the coming of the kingdom of God via societal change apart from confession of Christ."[11] Although he believes salvation is vertical and horizontal, personal and social, he believes it should nevertheless be restricted to the confession of Christ as Lord. As such "salvation language should probably not be used to refer to the imperfect emergence of justice and peace in society at large before the return of Christ." He concludes: "If biblical usage is decisive, then we should use salvation language to refer only to what happens when persons confess Christ, experience the salvation he offers, and begin to live out the radical demands of his new kingdom."[12]

We must not confuse the ultimate hope of a new creation with proximate hopes, hopes of change in our neighborhood, society, or world. Too often the language of Christian hope is used of hopes for change in history. Christians are people of hope, it is said, and such hope can energize movements for social change. But this confuses biblical hope for a new creation with hope for a change in society. It cannot be sustained in the light of the biblical evidence. The eschatological future hope is certain and arises from the promise of God. It does not disappoint us (Rom. 5:5). Historical hopes *are* susceptible to disappointment.

God is sovereignly working throughout the world. This is what the Reformed tradition calls "common grace." "[Your Father] makes his sun rise on the evil and on the good, and sends rain on the just and on the unjust" (Matt. 5:45). Howard Peskett suggests it is better to speak of "reforming" society rather than "redeeming" society.[13] Because God is active in the world, we can attempt social

---

[11] Ronald J. Sider with James Parker, "How Broad Is Salvation in Scripture?" in *In Word and Deed*, ed. Bruce Nicholls (Carlisle, UK: Paternoster, 1985), 104. This represents a modification of Sider's previous stance in Ronald J. Sider, "Evangelism, Salvation and Social Justice," *International Review of Mission* 64:255 (1975): 251–67 and in Sider and Stott, *Evangelism, Salvation and Social Justice*.
[12] Sider, "How Broad Is Salvation in Scripture?" 105.
[13] Howard Peskett and Vinoth Ramachandra, *The Message of Mission* (Nottingham, UK: Inter-Varsity, 2003), 255.

reform. But society will not be redeemed until Christ returns. We should not call social change the coming of the kingdom of God. God's sovereignty did not start with the incarnation. God has always been active in history. But the coming of Jesus represented something new: the coming of Jesus meant that "the kingdom of God has come upon you" (Luke 11:20; see also Mark 1:14–15; Luke 17:20–21). The kingdom of God is God's reestablishing his rule over a world. God's coming kingdom is present now through Spirit and the gospel where the rule of God and his Messiah are acknowledged. In other words, the church is the "place" on earth where God rules and which anticipates, albeit imperfectly, the future kingdom of God that will encompass all creation. "The New Testament presents the church as the community of the kingdom in which Jesus is acknowledged as Lord of the universe and through which, in anticipation of the end, the kingdom is concretely manifested in history."[14] It is the church that makes manifest the eternal reconciling purposes of God (Eph. 3:1–11).

Summary

Some Christians see advances in social justice in history as the coming of God's kingdom, but in the New Testament the kingdom comes through the gospel as people submit to God's Word. God's kingdom will be supreme over all things when Christ returns, but in the meantime it comes secretly and graciously through God's Word. The social dimension of salvation is anticipated in history in the life of the Christian community.

---

[14] C. René Padilla, *Mission between the Times* (Grand Rapids, MI: Eerdmans, 1985), 189–90.

Good News
to the Poor

Jesus describes the gospel as "good news" for the poor (Luke 7:22). He says that he came "to proclaim good news to the poor" (Luke 4:18). This chapter explores what it means to say that the gospel is good news *to the poor* in particular. In doing so we will see the social and political dimension to the gospel.

1) A Message of Liberation

The gospel is good news to the poor because the reign of God is a reign of justice and peace in which the last will be first and the first will be last. The gospel directs our attention to the wonderful future that God has promised us in Christ. But that is especially good news for those who do not experience this life as one of blessing. Indeed, time and again Luke speaks of a reversal at the end of time, and he speaks of it in social and political categories. Mary sings: "He has brought down the mighty from their thrones and exalted those of humble estate; he has filled the hungry with good things, and the rich he has sent away empty" (Luke 1:52–53). It is no surprise to find that so many of the Negro spirituals express this longing for the new future that God promises.

Five centuries before the coming of Jesus, God had judged the Jewish nation by allowing them to be defeated by the Babylonians and to be taken away into exile. Seventy years later, under the leadership of Ezra and Nehemiah, some of the Jews had returned to the land. But the exile was not really over. They were not free in their land. The land was still under the control of other nations (Neh. 9:36–37). Moreover, the underlying problems of the exile had not been dealt with: the problems of people's sin and God's judgment. The Jews of Jesus's day viewed Roman occupation in this way: they had been conquered and enslaved by the nations, and the Promised Land had been defiled by Gentile occupation. They were looking for God to intervene to liberate his people and end the exile.

In 167 BC the Syrian ruler Antiochus Epiphanes desecrated the temple in Jerusalem and dedicated it to the worship of himself. He provoked a rebellion led by Judas Maccabaeus. On December 15, 164 BC, three years after its desecration, Judas Maccabaeus cleansed and restored the temple. A new festival—the festival of Hanukkah—was added to commemorate this act of liberation. God had intervened to vindicate his people and his honor. And this act deeply shaped the identity of the Jews for the next two hundred years. With God's help they had thrown out an occupying army that had desecrated the land and the temple.

So when in 63 BC the Romans conquered Judea, there was a series of violent revolts and revolutions. At first the Romans ruled through the descendants of Judas Maccabaeus (the liberators became the collaborators) and then through Herod the Great and his sons. In Jesus's day the Sadducees were the religious elite while the Herodians represented the political elite. They opted for compromise, for political submission to the Roman Empire from which they therefore benefited. In 4 BC, as Herod the Great lay dying, some Jews pulled down the ornamental eagle he had placed over the temple gate. One of Herod the Great's final acts was to punish them severely. Then, in the power vacuum created by his death, there followed a series of rebellions, including one in which two thousand rebels were crucified. In 6 AD Judas the Galilean led a revolt against Rome. Although the rebellion was crushed, the aspirations of the movement continued. Those sympathetic to it were called "zealots." One of Jesus's disciples was Simon the Zealot (Luke 6:15).

Throughout the next seventy years there were regular revolts and riots. We know about one of the minor ones because its leader, Barabbas, was released by Pontius Pilate at Passover instead of Jesus (Mark 15:7). Two of the sons of Judas the Galilean were crucified in AD 46 for rebellion. In the AD 50s there was a group called the Sicarii, "the dagger-men," known for their practice of knifing people they considered to be collaborators with the Roman rulers. Around this time an Egyptian Jew assembled several thousand people on the Mount of Olives, claiming that the walls of Jerusalem would fall as the walls of Jericho had done and that they would march in to take the city back from the Romans. In fact, his followers were massacred. "Revolution of one sort or another was in the air, and often present on the ground . . . throughout the period of Roman rule. Whenever it was suppressed in one place it sprang up in another."[1] There were economic and political pressures behind these rebellions, but they were also theological acts done with the expectation that God would intervene to liberate his people.

Not everyone thought that the answer was violent rebellion. The Pharisees believed that if you could not cleanse the land, then you could at least cleanse yourself. So they advocated ritual purity. The Pharisees worked with the establishment as a kind of pressure group, calling it to be true to the traditions of the nation. But their concern with personal ritual purity became a kind of symbolic act of resistance to Roman defilement. The land may not be clean, but you could be clean within the land. Their hope was that by purifying the people they might prepare the way for God's intervention.

Then there were the Essenes. The Essenes were made famous by the discovery in 1947 of the Dead Sea Scrolls that were written by them. They separated themselves from society into separate communities, including the community at Qumran where the

---

[1] N. T. Wright, *The New Testament and the People of God* (London: SPCK, 1992), 176.

Dead Sea Scrolls were found. They believed the nation of Israel was corrupt—particularly its rulers who colluded with the Gentiles who defiled the land—but the rest of the nation was also blind. They were waiting for God to act, to send his anointed king and priest to lead a great war against the Sons of Darkness. The Gentiles and the faithless Jews would be expelled and the Sons of Light would reign for a thousand years. True worship would be restored in a new temple. In the meantime, God had begun to act by calling the Essene community into existence. They were God's faithful people in waiting, waiting for the day of his coming justice.

This is the context in which Jesus operated, a context of occupation, revolution, and political ferment. And it is in this context that Jesus says he is bringing the exile to an end. What he says is explosive. The longed-for liberation is happening. Through Jesus, God is intervening in history in faithfulness to his covenant promises.

This emphasis is clear in the opening chapters of Matthew's Gospel. Matthew opens his Gospel by recounting the genealogy of Jesus. He structures it into three groups of fourteen to highlight Jesus's link to Abraham, David, and the exile. Jesus is the one who will fulfil the promises to Abraham and who will reign on the throne of King David, but he is also the one who brings an end to the Babylonian exile. In 2:18 Matthew quotes from Jeremiah 31:15, a prophecy concerning the end of exile. Likewise in 3:1–3 Matthew quotes from Isaiah 40:1–3 where Isaiah promises "comfort" to the exiles. Israel had first entered the land through the River Jordan, quite literally passing through it. So the baptism of Jesus in the Jordan (Matt. 3:13) was symbolic of reentering the land. In 4:12–16 Matthew again applies a prophecy about the end of exile (Isa. 9:1–2) to the ministry of Jesus.

In the Old Testament the end of the exile that Israel longed for was often described in terms of the exodus. The exodus was God's great act of liberation in Israel's history, freeing the people from slavery and oppression in Egypt. Now they looked for a new exodus. And Matthew presents the liberation of Jesus as a new exodus. Jesus comes out of Egypt (2:13–15). Israel is first called God's son when Moses goes to Pharaoh to demand that he let the people go free. Now the voice from heaven says of Jesus, "This is my beloved Son" (Matt. 3:17). Jesus is tempted in the wilderness for forty days just as Israel was tempted in the wilderness for forty years (4:1–2). Israel failed the test, but Jesus is the faithful one. The book of Deuteronomy was the word Moses spoke to the people on the verge of the Promised Land, and now Jesus counters Satan with words from Deuteronomy (4:3–11).

This theme continues into the Sermon on the Mount. This is the background to the so-called Beatitudes. The blessings promised in the Beatitudes arise because God's people will once again live in the land of blessing, the land flowing with milk and honey. They will be restored to life under the reign of God (Matt. 5:3). They will receive the comfort promised to the exiles in Isaiah 40:1–3 (Matt. 5:4). Matthew 5:5 is a reference to Psalm 37:11, which says, "The meek shall inherit the land and delight themselves in abundant peace." It is a promise of inheriting the land, so, in this context, of returning from exile, except that Jesus now has the whole earth in mind as the home of God's people. To thirst for righteousness is to long for God's saving intervention in history, and to be satisfied is to enjoy the land of milk and honey again. "Sons of God" is what Israel was called when Moses demanded that Pharaoh set them free; the final plague falls on Egypt's firstborn because Egypt would not liberate God's "firstborn" (see Ex. 4:22–23). So to be called "sons of God" is to be the liberated ones. The Beatitudes are not spiritual aphorisms, nor guides to a happy life, nor moral precepts; they are announcements of liberation. They are announcing a return to the land of blessing—except that the land has become the whole earth.

Who is it that will enjoy this liberation? Who will enjoy the blessings of the Promised Land? Not the politically powerful (the Sadducees and the Herodians), for blessed are the meek (Matt. 5:5). Not the violent revolutionaries (the Zealots), for blessed are the merciful and the peacemakers (vv. 7, 9; see also vv. 39, 41, 44).

Not the religiously pure (the Pharisees), for "blessed are the poor in spirit and the pure *in heart*" (vv. 3, 8). Not those who separate themselves (the Essenes), for the blessed ones are a city on a hill and a light that cannot be hidden (vv. 14–15). No, the ones who enjoy liberation are the poor in spirit, the broken people. People sometimes say that to proclaim liberation ignores the fact that the poor are sinners too. But Jesus suggests an opposite problem. Broken people know they are broken. What they struggle to grasp is that God welcomes people like them. The bigger problem is with the "sorted out" people; they are the ones who struggle to recognize the depth of their sin and the poverty of their spirit.

Reading the Sermon on the Mount in the light of its context highlights the radical power of the message of Jesus. It reveals its social and political cutting edge. But does it also make it remote to our concerns? People today do not long for a return from Babylonian exile. We are not under Roman occupation. What is the contemporary relevance of Jesus's message of liberation?

The answer is that people today still long for liberation. They long for liberation from the knock of the loan shark, from dependency on drugs, from the bottle, from cycles of violence, from the threat of a poor harvest, from the fear of corrupt officials. We live in a society of broken people needing liberation and longing for home. This message of liberation speaks directly to our situation.

The exile in Babylon was a picture of humanity's exile from God. In the first half of Ezekiel the prophet warns the first wave of exiles of God's judgment against his people—Jerusalem and the temple will be destroyed. He has two repeated refrains: "Then they will know that I am the Lord" and "I am against you." In chapters 25–32 Ezekiel addresses the surrounding nations, and the message to the nations is the *same message* as the message to Israel with the same refrains. The nations will discover that *Israel's God is their God.* They, too, "will know that I am the Lord" (25:7, 11, 14, 17; 26:6, 23, 24; 29:9, 16, 21; 30:8, 19, 25, 26; 32:15). And the nations will discover that *Israel's fate will be their fate.* The nations are told: "I am against you" (26:3; 28:22; 29:3, 10; 30:22). The exile in Babylon is a picture of humanity's fate, exiled from the blessing and peace of God's loving reign.

Jesus proclaimed a message of liberation. It is a political message, not in the sense of fomenting revolution now (see Matt. 5:9, 39, 41, 44) but in the sense of witnessing to the hidden revolution that will be revealed at the last day. It is a message of *future* liberation. But the new regime has begun among Christ's community of the broken. The Christian community is the place of liberation.

2) A Message of Grace

The second reason why the gospel is described as good news to the poor is that it is a message of grace. Salvation is dependent solely upon God's grace. It is not dependent upon wealth, status, or power, so the poor are not excluded. With nothing to lose, the poor do not need to go through the eye of a needle to enter the kingdom of God (Luke 18:25). Moreover, by making them children of God, the gospel gives the poor a dignity that the world denies them. Asked what the gospel had done for his people, an indigenous Christian leader from northern Argentina replied that "it had enabled them to look the white person fully in the eye."[2] Time and again the gospel has brought about social and economic changes in communities by giving the poor dignity and direction. And the gospel has done this even when this was not a goal of those who brought the gospel to the community. Bible translation is just one example of this. Translating the Bible into the languages of indigenous cultures has repeatedly given marginalized peoples a renewed sense of the value of their culture and identity.[3]

In the West it seems we are obsessed with celebrities. We have magazines and television programs devoted to them. Often when a major news story is breaking, the front pages of our newspapers are full of the antics of celebrities. Half the time we cannot remember why someone became a celebrity, but that does not seem to mat-

---

[2] Andrew Kirk, *What Is Mission? Theological Explorations* (London: DLT, 1999), 71.
[3] See Dewi A. Hughes, *Castrating Culture: A Christian Perspective on Ethnic Identity for the Margins* (Carlisle, UK: Paternoster, 2001).

ter. In the church it is the same. We love our celebrity converts. Sportsmen, singers, models—if they become Christians, then we buy their books, go to their concerts, trumpet their conversion. Best of all we love to show them off to unbelievers. We put on meetings where they give their testimony. I guess we think that people we know are more likely to believe if they discover that a famous person has become a Christian. A famous name gives credibility to the gospel. It makes Christianity cool. Or at least that is what we think. When we engage with the world, we try to convince people that we are worthy of being listened to because we are respectable. We hide away the freaks, the mentally unstable, the socially inept, the people who smell, the people who stand too close when they talk to you, the poor people, the stupid people. After all, no one is going to listen to them. Instead we put out the well-spoken, well-dressed, well-mannered people and say, "Look, listen to us, we're okay."

But Paul takes a very different line in 1 Corinthians 1:26–31. Paul has been expounding his claim that "the word of the cross is folly to those who are perishing, but to us who are being saved it is the power of God" (v. 18). God, he says, destroys the wisdom of the world by revealing his power in something that worldly wisdom does not recognize (vv. 19–22). It seems as if only powerful signs can impress Jews and as if only clever philosophical ideas can impress the Greeks. But we must not place our confidence in these, says Paul. We must not think that doing miracles or expounding clever arguments will convert the world, because the power of God and the wisdom of God are found in the message of the cross (vv. 23–25). Our message must be, and can only be, Christ crucified. When we preach Christ crucified, the Jews will be offended and the Greeks will laugh at us. But we have no choice, for we have no other message. Only the message of Christ crucified is truly power and truly wisdom.

In verses 26–31 Paul extends his argument. God has made foolish the wisdom of the world in the cross; now he is doing it among his people. Paul invites the Corinthians to look at themselves. They do not represent the wise, influential, and noble people of this world. There were some in Corinth like this but not many. The church was primarily made up of those who were on the fringe, those in society who did not have much to appeal to. God is choosing these kinds of people to be part of his demonstration of the wisdom of the cross. God chooses the foolish, weak, and lowly to nullify human power and wisdom. He shames wisdom, power, and status because we use these things to proclaim that we do not need God. They all express the rebellion in Eden. But God makes a habit of choosing the foolish, weak, and despised people of the world to demonstrate that salvation is all of his grace. He leaves no room for us to boast in our wisdom or strength. Our boast, our only boast, is in Jesus (vv. 30–31).

In the area in which I live, the affluent, respectable British people are not interested in the gospel. The people who respond to the gospel are the socially marginalized, the displaced, the refugees. It is true today on a global scale. The church in the West is in decline, while the church in the Third World is growing. The balance of power in the Christian world is shifting to Africa and Latin America. Perhaps God is doing this to shame the economic and military power and the academic, rationalistic wisdom of the West. And not only that—perhaps he is doing it to shame the power and wisdom of the Western church.

Jesus expounds these themes of liberation and grace with explosive force in Luke 18.

> And he told them a parable to the effect that they ought always to pray and not lose heart. He said, "In a certain city there was a judge who neither feared God nor respected man. And there was a widow in that city who kept coming to him and saying, "Give me justice against my adversary." For a while he refused, but afterward he said to himself, "Though I neither fear God nor respect man, yet because this widow keeps bothering me, I will give her justice, so that she will not beat me down by her continual coming." And the Lord said, "Hear what the unrighteous judge says. And will not God give justice to his elect, who cry to him day and night? Will he delay long over them? I tell you, he

will give justice to them speedily. Nevertheless, when the Son of Man comes, will he find faith on earth?"

He also told this parable to some who trusted in themselves that they were righteous, and treated others with contempt: "Two men went up into the temple to pray, one a Pharisee and the other a tax collector. The Pharisee, standing by himself, prayed thus: 'God, I thank you that I am not like other men, extortioners, unjust, adulterers, or even like this tax collector. I fast twice a week; I give tithes of all that I get.' But the tax collector, standing far off, would not even lift up his eyes to heaven, but beat his breast, saying, 'God, be merciful to me, a sinner!' I tell you, this man went down to his house justified, rather than the other. For everyone who exalts himself will be humbled, but the one who humbles himself will be exalted." (vv. 1–14)

This is usually called "the parable of the *persistent* widow." The message seems to be that if we keep on asking God for something, then eventually he will give us what we want. But the point of the parable is that God is *not* like the judge. God does *not* need to be nagged into submission. He is the God who *does* care for widows. "The Lord watches over the sojourners; he upholds the widow and the fatherless, but the way of the wicked he brings to ruin" (Ps. 146:9). Indeed Jesus says at the conclusion of the parable that God gives justice "speedily" (Luke 18:8). In fact, in verse 14 a man who has cried out to God for mercy "went down to his house justified." He receives justice before he has even got home. God, we discover, gives justice and vindication even before the end of history. When Luke tells us in verse 1 that the meaning of the parable is that we "should always pray and not give up," he does not mean that we should persist in prayer until we get what we want. Literally it means: "always to pray and not lose heart" (v. 1). This is a parable about not being discouraged, not about losing faith in God. Jesus himself says the parable is about faith (v. 8). Prayer is taken as an example of faith, because in our experience prayer is the supreme expression of faith. Prayer is faith articulated. So it is a parable about *perseverance* rather than *persistence*.

But this parable is not about trusting God in some general sense. It is about trusting God for something in particular. The parable uses the language of justice. The widow's petition is: "Give me justice against my adversary" (v. 3). The judge eventually responds: "Because this widow keeps bothering me, I will give her justice" (v. 5). And Jesus says the meaning is this: "Will not God give justice to his elect, who cry to him day and night? Will he delay long over them? I tell you, he will give justice to them speedily" (vv. 7–8). The preceding section is about the coming of God's kingdom and the return of the Son of Man (17:20–37). Waiting patiently for Christ's return means not being fooled by those who say Christ has already returned—no one will mistake his coming when it happens (17:22–25). In the meantime the disciples are to pray for the coming of Christ and not lose heart (18:1). The challenge is not to lose faith in the coming of Christ (v. 8). But in this parable the return of Christ is spoken of as justice for God's *chosen ones.*

It is not just the parable of the widow that is about justice. The next parable is also about justice (vv. 9–14). It is addressed "to some who trusted in themselves that they were righteous" (v. 9). *Righteousness* and *justice* are the same word in Greek, so this parable is addressed to those who were confident in their own justice. And at the end of the parable, the tax collector goes "down to his house justified" (v. 14). He receives justice. He is vindicated. In Psalm 143 the psalmist says: "Hear my prayer, O Lord; give ear to my pleas for mercy! In your faithfulness answer me, in your righteousness. . . . For your name's sake, O Lord, preserve my life! In your righteousness bring my soul out of trouble! And in your steadfast love you will cut off my enemies, and you will destroy all the adversaries of my soul, for I am your servant" (Ps. 143:1, 11–12). The psalmist cries out to God for justice, for God to act in righteousness. And that means delivering the psalmist from his enemies. To cry to God for justice and to appeal to God's righteousness is to ask God to intervene to rescue his people, to vindicate them, and to judge their enemies. The psalmist calls upon God to intervene in the dispute between God's people and God's enemies and to vindicate his people. This will be God acting in saving righteousness.

With all of this the Jewish leaders would have been fine. They would have agreed. This is what they expected. Verses 1–8a fit with Jewish expectation. They expected that one day God would intervene in history to liberate them from their enemies. They were looking for the day when God would establish them once again as free people in a free land—as God's people in God's land. The *Zealots* expected God to liberate his people as they fomented revolution. As they rose up in violent revolt, God would act in saving righteousness and establish justice for his faithful ones. The *Pharisees* hoped that by ritual cleansing, by fasting, by repentance for the past, by adherence to the Law, they would show themselves to be God's faithful people waiting for God's liberation. The *Essenes* thought they were the true Israel who had separated themselves from the corruption and compromise going on around them. They and they alone were the true faithful people of God. What the Zealots, the Pharisees, and the Essenes all agreed on is that God would come to establish justice for his faithful people. God would vindicate his faithful people. They disagreed on how it would come about—maybe through violent revolution, maybe through ritual purification, maybe through separation—but they all agreed it would happen and that they, as God's faithful people, would be the beneficiaries.

With this background in mind we can begin to appreciate the explosive quality of Jesus's concluding words to the parable. "I tell you, he will give justice to them speedily. Nevertheless, when the Son of Man comes, will he find faith on earth?" (Luke 18:8). Everything is fine up to this point. The religious leaders are with Jesus all the way. Zealots, Pharisees, and Essenes would all have agreed with the idea of God coming to establish justice for his people. But the final question is like a grenade thrown into the picture. It is like one of those films in which a bomb is thrown and everything goes quiet. All you can hear is the sound of the bomb rolling on the ground and coming to a halt. Then boom. In this case the explosion takes place in the next parable, the parable of the Pharisees and the tax collector. For the moment, let us watch the bomb rolling across the floor with the metal clinking on the hard floor. What Jesus questions is whether his hearers are in fact God's faithful people. Are these the ones who will receive justice and vindication? Could it be that they are not God's faithful people? When God comes in justice to bring vindication, could it be that he will not come to the Zealots or the Pharisees or the Essenes? He may have to look elsewhere to find his faithful people. For the mark of the elect is not their ethnic identity. Nor is it their religious identity. The mark of the elect is that they cry out to God day and night for mercy: "And will not God give justice to his elect, who cry to him day and night?" (v. 7). The chosen ones of God seek his mercy. They look *to God* for justice, not to their racial identity, or their good works, or their religion.

In the parable of the Pharisee and the tax collector (vv. 9–14) Jesus redefines the justice of God and who receives it. Jesus tells the story of two men. One is the ideal Israelite: zealous, righteous, religious. But he does not receive justice. And then there is a sinner, one of the despised, a traitor, a collaborator with the Romans. But when he cries out to God for mercy he receives justice—just as Jesus promised in verse 6. He goes home justified (vv. 13–14). God saving his people involves something greater than liberation from Roman occupation: he will free them from the underlying problems of sin, death, and judgment. The faithful people whom God vindicates are not the politically zealous nor the religiously pure but those who cry out to God for mercy.

Taken together these parables teach us:

1) To look to God for liberation and justice. When Christ returns, God will establish his righteousness. He will reign once again over the world in justice. He will save and vindicate his people. He will bring down rulers and lift up the humble. He will fill the hungry with good things but send the rich away empty (Luke 1:51–53). This is good news for the poor.

2) To not lose heart. Liberation and justice are not our experience now. We cry out to God to end suffering, injustice, and the dishonor in which his name is held, but often God does not intervene. And so Jesus tells us not to lose heart, to keep faith until the Son of Man comes (vv. 1, 8). If we stop praying, then we portray God as worse than the unjust judge. The unjust judge gives justice in the end, even though he "neither feared God nor respected man" (v. 2). So if we lose faith in God and give up praying, then we make God out to be worse than the unjust judge who at least granted justice eventually.

3) To look to God for justification. God also gives justice "speedily." The tax collector receives justice before he goes home. Justice is a present experience for those who cry out to God for mercy. God's coming in justice will mean judgment to all people, for none is righteous. But when we turn to God in faith, he justifies us. He declares us to be just and guiltless— even though we are guilty. Psalm 143 not only pictures a court case between God's people and God's nations in which God intervenes to vindicate his people; it also pictures a court case between God and his people. If this case is brought to judgment, then God will be vindicated through our condemnation because "no one living is righteous before you" (Ps. 143:2). But God has brought this case to judgment in the cross. He has condemned his Son so that he can declare us just at the same time as vindicating his justice (see Rom. 3:21–26). Through God's grace we become part of the community of the faithful ones who can look to God's coming vindication with hope and confidence.

Some Christians want to reduce Christianity to a message of personal piety and individual salvation. Others go to the other extreme, reducing Christianity to a message of political liberation or liberal causes. Neither does justice to the good news proclaimed by Jesus.

We can and should proclaim the good news of liberation to the poor. We can and should promise them a kingdom of justice, peace, and blessing. We should express this in terms that connect with their experience of slavery and oppression. But we cannot and should not promise too much. To proclaim liberation within history is to promise what we cannot deliver. Liberation is a future reality. In the meantime we are not to lose heart. We are to keep faith with God.

3) A Message of Community

But it is not only in the future that the poor experience the good news. Through the gospel, the poor become part of a community of love and care. Justice is a present experience for the people of God.

We have seen how the Beatitudes in the Sermon on the Mount should be read as an announcement of liberation and an end to exile. Jesus continues by saying, "You are the salt of the earth" (Matt. 5:13). He is talking to his disciples (v. 1). Salt in the Old Testament was a sign of covenant faithfulness. In the Old Testament salt was to be added to every sacrifice (Lev. 2:13). The reason given is that salt is a sign of the covenant with God. Numbers talks of "a covenant of salt forever before the Lord for you and your offspring with you" (Num. 18:19; see also Ex. 30:35). Salt is a sign that the covenant will last, a sign of covenant faithfulness. Adding salt was a way of saying: "I bind myself to the agreement." It was our equivalent of shaking on it. This was how the contract was signed. Still today some Arabs throw salt to seal an agreement. "Ought you not to know that the Lord God of Israel gave the kingship over Israel forever to David and his sons by a covenant of salt?" (2 Chron. 13:5). Salt was a sign that the covenant would last forever. It was sign of faithfulness and commitment.

So when Jesus says, "You are the salt of the earth," he is not saying they were to act as a preservative, upholding the morality of society. Rather, Jesus is saying to his followers: "You are the faithful ones; you are the ones who are part of the covenant." When he talks about salt losing its saltiness, he is talking about the nation of Israel. They have not been faithful to the covenant, so they will not enjoy liberation from exile. They have been and will be "thrown out"; in other words, they have been exiled. They have been and will be "trampled under people's feet" (Matt. 5:13); in other words, they have been judged by a conquering army.

Remember the context. The place is crawling with Roman soldiers and Roman officials enforcing Roman rule. The country is full of Jews longing for liberation and an end to exile. And Jesus says: you are the salt of the earth, the light of the world, a city on a hill (5:13–16). You are the liberated community. You are the new society. You are the radical alternative. Commenting on Colossians, Vinoth Ramachandra says:

> The proof that God's future is already impinging on the present is found in the little communities . . . where men and women have been set free from their "estrangement and hostility" (Col. 1:21). These are communities of "hope," a foretaste of the reconciliation to come. It is through their gospel living (Col. 1:10) and gospel preaching (Col. 1:27) that the cosmic goal of renewal and transformation will be accomplished.[4]

For now we go on living under the old regimes of this world. But a new regime has begun. A revolution has taken place. The old ways of oppression are coming to an end. A new community with a new government has begun. It operates secretly in the midst of this world. It is a community that offers peace and justice.

In the Lord's Prayer Jesus says: "Forgive us our sins, for we ourselves forgive everyone who is indebted to us" (Luke 11:4). God's forgiveness of us in the future is related to our forgiveness of others in the present. It is not that we can earn forgiveness by being forgiving. It is rather that our experience of God's great mercy should makes us merciful people (Matt. 18:21–35; 1 John 3:16–17). The experience of grace transforms us into gracious people. It is not just about interpersonal conflict. It is about how we treat other people. It is about economic generosity. While God forgives our *sins*, we forgive our *debtors*. Luke could have used the

---

[4] Howard Peskett and Vinoth Ramachandra, *The Message of Mission* (Nottingham, UK: Inter-Varsity, 2003), 31.

word *sin* in both cases, but he chose to highlight the economic implications of Jesus's words. John Howard Yoder argues that Jesus announced an eschatological jubilee when he proclaimed "the year of the Lord's favour" (Luke 4:19).[5] In the Old Testament Year of Jubilee, debts were forgiven and slaves were set free as the people celebrated God's grace to them in providing atonement (see Leviticus 25 and Deuteronomy 15). Now the Lamb of God, who takes away the sins of the world, has come. In the light of God's forgiveness, a new era of economic and social relations has begun among those forgiven and set free by Christ's death.[6] The followers of Jesus are to live as both recipients of, and participants in, a permanent jubilee.[7]

Jim Wallis describes the Open Door Community as "a community of hospitality and justice for the poor" in Atlanta, Georgia. "On Sunday nights, when Murphy gets out her guitar, everybody sings together in a service that unites those who were never intended, in this world, to worship God together. But they do, and every time I am there I experience a little bit of heaven right in the midst of our still-divided earth. Communities like the Open Door provide us with both a sign and a promise."[8] The Christian community is both a sign and a promise of God's coming liberation. We are the presence of God's liberating kingdom in a broken world. We are the place where liberation can be found, offering a home for exiled people. We are to welcome the broken people to a community of broken people. We are the community among whom liberation is a present reality—the jubilee people who live with new economic and social relationships. We are the light of the world, a city on a hill. The challenge for us is to articulate Jesus's message of liberation in a way that connects with people's experience and offers a place of liberation in the Christian community.

---

[5] See John Howard Yoder, *The Politics of Jesus* (Grand Rapids, MI: Eerdmans, 1972), 34–39, 64–77.
[6] Tom Wright, *The Lord and His Prayer* (Oxford, UK: Triangle, 1996), 51–56.
[7] See Tim Chester, *The Message of Prayer* (Nottingham, UK: Inter-Varsity, 2003), 168–70.
[8] Jim Wallis, *The Soul of Politics* (New York: Fount, 1994), 77–78.

Summary

The gospel is good news to the poor because it is:

- a message of liberation—the gospel is the promise of liberation from all those things, personal and social, that enslave us;
- a message of grace—God's promise of forgiveness and liberation does not depend on our status, education, or wealth;
- a message of community—the coming liberation of God is anticipated in the liberating relationships of the Christian community.

"Land of Milk and Honey"

Stewart Henderson

As much as anything else, the following poem by Stewart Hender-son has helped me make the connection between Jesus's message of liberation to the marginalized people of first-century Palestine and my own experience of church planting. Using the language of God's covenant promises, Henderson powerfully evokes the need for liberation and the longing for home experienced by many today. Just as the people of Jesus's day longed for liberation, so people today long for liberation from "a gaunt consumer cul-de-sac . . . the loan shark's knock . . . glass confetti . . . [and] demons of despon-dency." We are still far from the land of milk of honey. Yet, as he puts it, "heaven lingers in these sides streets." The Christian com-munity is the sign and presence of liberation in a broken world.

Is this the land of milk and honey,
the one for which this city gave
conscripted youth to war's dark waters,
woodbine battalions of the brave?

This city of abandoned vehicles,
bankrupt stock and playtime crack,
a promised land of little promise,
a gaunt consumer cul-de-sac.

When we were young Orwell, Priestley,
chastened us with postcards home,
writing of a TB kingdom,
a cloth-capped land of monochrome.

And as for their HP descendants,
cocooned in space with satellite,
not knowing of the word "redemption",
owned by the loan shark's knock at night.

Is this the land of milk and honey
where birdsong seldom cleans the air
and all around is glass confetti
and only strangers pause to stare?

Absorbed into the local spirits:
demons of despondency;
souls and bodies soaked in debt,
crying out for jubilee.

Yet heaven lingers in these side streets
amidst the metal shutter shops
where lethal games played with syringes
have long replaced kids' spinning tops.

And heaven lodges in these side streets,
feeling each tormenting pain,
counting out each tranquillizer,
visiting the barely sane.

This is a land of milk and honey
and perpetual alarms,
full of light and sawn-off menace,
a daily paradox of psalms.

This is a land of milk and honey,
bereft of bud and bursting leaves;
though glory may not seem apparent,
a place where Jesus lives and breathes.[1]

---

[1] Used with permission of the author. Woodbines were a popular brand of cigarette during World War I. The writers George Orwell and J. B. Priestly powerfully described working class poverty in the early twentieth century.

7

Good News
to the Rich

People do not think they are rich. Most people think of the rich as those who have more than they do. And if they receive a pay increase or inherit some wealth, then the definition rises accordingly. The rich are always other people—never us. But consider your answer to the following question: how many taps do you have in your house providing clean water, hot and cold? Remember to include the washing machine if you have one and any outside taps for the garden. If your answer is one or more, then you are among the richest seventh of the world's population in economic terms.

One-third of deaths—eighteen million people a year—are caused by poverty. Every year more than ten million children die of hunger and preventable diseases. Over one billion people live on less than one dollar a day with nearly half the world's population—2.8 billion people—surviving on less than two dollars.[1]

Yet many of us have become morally numb to these facts. Something is not right. How you handle your money is important for your spiritual well-being. "No one can serve two masters," said Jesus, "for either he will hate the one and love the other, or he will be devoted to the one and despise the other. You cannot serve God and money" (Matt. 6:24). During the crusades it is said

---

[1] http://www.guardian.co.uk/politics/2005/may/15/uk.g81.

the mercenaries were baptized holding their swords above the water—they did not want Christ to control their swords. And so it is with our wallets; perhaps we should hold them above the water when we are baptized! But Jesus says that we cannot serve money *and* God. Money is dangerous. If you do not master money, it will master you.

The average American sees two million television commercials by the time he reaches the age of sixty-five, and our children watch twenty thousand commercials each year.[2] That means most of us spend more time exposed to the message of advertisements than the message of God's Word. So which is going to have the biggest impact on our worldview?

Christians give on average just 2 percent of their income.[3] John Calvin said: "All that the church possesses, either in lands or in money, is the inheritance of the poor." Those who handle church wealth should do so remembering that it is "appointed for the need of the poor," and to keep it from the poor or waste it is to "be guilty of blood." Calvin goes on to describe an imaginary conversation in which God rebukes those who did not use church property and ornaments to relieve the plight of the poor.[4]

So how we handle our money is vital for our spiritual well-being. Every time we spend money, we are making an ethical decision. We are deciding not to spend it on helping the poor or furthering the gospel. For me the struggle was typified by tea shops. Surely every trip to a tea shop is in some sense a crime against humanity? After all, I could have a cup of tea at home for a fraction of the price. That may seem laughable, but I want you to see the force of such a view. The philosopher Peter Singer asks his students, If you pass a child drowning in the pond should you do anything? They all say, "Yes." Even if it means getting dirty and missing lectures? "Yes, you should still do it." Does it make a difference that others are able to help? "No." Would it make a difference if the child were

---

[2] http://www.csun.edu/science/health/docs/tv&health.html.
[3] David B. Barrett, Tom M. Johnson, and Peter F. Crossing, "Missiometrics: Creating Your Own Analysis of Global Data," *International Bulletin of Missionary Research* 31:1 (2007), 8.
[4] John Calvin, *Institutes*, 4.4.6–8.

in a far-off country? And here we hesitate, because, as Peter Singer points out, that is the situation we are all in, and it is not clear what moral difference lack of proximity makes.[5] At relatively little cost to ourselves we can help destitute children. Could you sit in the tea shop with starving children outside the window looking in? That is not a hypothetical situation in many Third World cities. And what about television pictures of destitute children?

When I worked for Tearfund we often used to say that we should not make people feel guilty, to which my friend Dewi Hughes would retort: "Yes, we should, for we are guilty!" John Calvin condemns "ostentatious banquets, bodily apparel and domestic architecture"—what we would call fancy dinner parties, designer gear, and an obsession with home improvements. "All these things are defended under the pretext of Christian freedom," he continues. "They say that these are things indifferent. I admit it, provided they are used indifferently. But when they are coveted too greedily, when they are proudly boasted of, when they are lavishly squandered, things that were of themselves otherwise lawful are certainly defiled by these vices."[6] Consider the sin of Sodom. We usually think of the sin of Sodom as sexual debauchery. But according to Ezekiel the sin of Sodom was that she "had pride, excess of food, and prosperous ease, but did not aid the poor and needy" (Ezek. 16:49). It was not even that the people of Sodom had caused the plight of the poor but simply that they were unconcerned. As Dewi would say, we are guilty, but as Christians we have a remedy for guilt: the gospel. We remedy guilt by confessing our sins and finding consolation in the cross. We do not cope with guilt by denying our sin or downplaying the demands of discipleship.

Ray Bakke was speaking to a church about the need to care for the spiritual *and* physical needs of the urban poor. Someone asked, "Isn't that just the social gospel?" (The social gospel was, as we have

---

[5] Peter Singer, "Famine, Affluence, and Morality," *World Hunger and Moral Obligation*, ed. William Aiken and Hugh La Follette (Englewood Cliffs, NJ: Prentice-Hall, 1977), 22–36; and Peter Singer, *Practical Ethics*, 2nd ed. (Cambridge, UK: Cambridge University Press, 1993), 218–46.
[6] John Calvin, *The Institutes of Christian Religion*, trans. F. L. Battles, ed. J. T. McNeill (Philadelphia: Westminster/SCM, 1961), 3.19.9.

said, a movement that believed the kingdom of God could come in history through Christian social action.) So Ray Bakke asked: "Where do you live?" It was a pleasant neighborhood. "What is your house like?" It was a large house. "What car do you drive?" It was an up-market model. "What hopes do you have for your children?" And so it went on, until Ray Bakke said: "It seems to me that you are the one living out the social gospel."

Many of us live our lives as if material possessions matter most. Too often we are the ones who have made social factors key in determining our lives and our lifestyle. We are the ones who live the social gospel, not those trying to improve the lot of the poor. Through a thousand consumer choices we evangelicals have committed ourselves to a social gospel—not the social gospel of those who thought the kingdom of God could be established by social action but the social gospel of Western consumerism.

The Lie of Consumerism

Shopping is the religion of our age. Just look at shopping malls. Just as the medieval architects built cathedrals to glorify God, so we build wonderful shopping malls to glorify what we believe is important: shopping. The Meadowhall shopping mall, in Sheffield, where I live, even has a cathedral-like dome, while the Bentall Centre in Kingston-upon-Thames has a vast stained-glass window at one end. Alan Storkey warns that consumerism "is the chief rival to God in our culture." He recognizes that that may seem an odd claim: "It is, after all, just shopping." But:

> The faith lives and grows as myth because it has countless well-paid servants, who, though often unhappy, go about their Master's business. The servants of the Lord God are dwarfed in number and working hours by the servants of consumption. Its ability to recruit seems unlimited. Christianity, despite all the warnings in the gospels, has not even seen the challenge, the temptations, the lies, the enemy.[7]

[7] Alan Storkey, "Postmodernism Is Consumption," in *Christ and Consumerism: A Critical Analysis of the Spirit of the Age*, ed. Craig Bartholomew and Thorsten Moritz (Carlisle, UK: Paternoster, 2000), 101.

Not only has marketing taken on elements of religion; religion has taken on features of marketing. We *shop* for churches. And if we do not like the product, we move our business elsewhere. Just as people travel in their cars to shopping centers for the convenience and service they provide, so Christians drive past small, struggling churches to large mega-churches. Church has ceased to be a community of believers sharing their lives together and witnessing to their community. Instead it has become another product to be consumed at our convenience.

But the true preachers of this new religion are the media and the advertisers. They give us our values. United States spending on advertisements is around $144 billion a year.[8] And what they say we should value are material possessions. But Jesus said: "One's life does not consist in the abundance of his possessions" (Luke 12:15). The lie of consumerism is that we *can* find life, satisfaction, meaning, and fulfillment by buying consumer goods and services. Mike Starkey claims that advertisements are the "icons of Western consumer society." An icon embodies the values and ideals of a community. And the message of our modern advertising icons is "that consumption is the answer to a range of basic human questions. . . . Consumer advertising channels all our desires for a better world towards striving for consumer goods and personal prosperity."[9]

We actually ask, "How much is a person worth?" meaning, "What's their salary?" We measure worth in terms of how much somebody earns and how much they own. Alan Durning says of advertisements: "Even if they fail to sell a particular product, they sell consumerism itself by ceaselessly reiterating the idea that there is a product to solve each of life's problems, indeed that existence would be satisfying and complete if only we bought the right things."[10]

One recent advertisement for mobile phones typifies the message. An old mobile phone is shown covered in a paper bag. It is

---

[8] http://kantarmediana.com/intelligence/press/us-advertising-expenditures-increased-08-percent -2011.

[9] Mike Starkey, *Born to Shop* (Oxford, UK: Monarch, 1989), 37–38.

[10] Alan Durning, *How Much Is Enough: The Consumer Society and the Future of the Earth* (New York: Norton, 1992), 119.

too embarrassing to be seen, for it is out of date. The message is clear: without the latest gadget you are an embarrassment. Significance, security, purpose: all advertisements play upon one of these things, and their message is that they can be found in buying things, going out, having possessions. Consumer goods are what give meaning and satisfaction. "I shop, therefore I am."

And when we have not got the money, we do not let that stop us—after all, our very identity is at stake—so we borrow. Personal debt is a huge problem in the United States. In March 2012 the amount of outstanding consumer credit was $2,542 billion, and that excludes mortgages secured against real estate. That's over eight thousand dollars per person.[11] When money and possessions are so important to who you are—your sense of belonging, of being worth something—then not having it is a disaster. You have no choice but to borrow.

Consumerism tell us that the secret of life and happiness is to get more: more goods, more holidays, a better car. But this message is an illusion. It is an illusion because it does not give the full picture. It does not tell of the dark side of our consumerist culture: the pollution, the unemployment, the alienation and social breakdown. It does not tell us of the condition of the workers who make the products. But it is an illusion, too, because consumer goods do not bring fulfillment and satisfaction. In the United States people now consume twice as much as they did in the 1950s, yet research shows that people are not any happier than they were then.[12] In the United Kingdom, too, despite the highest income levels ever, researchers found many were profoundly unhappy. Fifty-five percent said they had felt depressed in the past year.[13] Psychologist Oliver James explains the role of advertising in the lives of the depressed: "They were led to believe that anything was possible. In reality, in the vast majority of cases, they still end up working very hard to make somebody else rich. And the advertisements

---

[11] http://www.federalreserve.gov/releases/g19/current/default.htm.
[12] Cited in Tom Sine, *Mustard vs. McWorld* (Oxford, UK: Monarch, 1999), 227.
[13] Ben Summerskill, *The Observer*, May 6, 2001.

which encouraged them to believe consumption was the root of all happiness have been strongly instrumental in creating discontent with their bodies and personalities."[14]

I sometimes do an exercise with groups in which we look at advertisements and ask what they promise. Here is the list from one set of advertisements: "power, peace, status, revival, a different dimension, paradise, values, a happy family life, performance, freedom, spirituality, comfort, enlightenment, friendship, the breath of life, reconciliation, identity, life, escape, balance, therapy, a future, insight." The extent of the lie is immediately apparent. These were advertisements for a brand of tea, a new mobile phone, a holiday destination, footwear, and so on. Self-evidently new shoes, a cup of tea, and a vacation in the sun cannot give you enlightenment, friendship, and identity let alone paradise and the breath of life! The work of groups like Adbusters ruthlessly exposes the false pretensions of advertising by creating mock advertisements that convey the real truth about products.[15] The lie of consumerism is that we can find satisfaction, meaning, and fulfillment by buying consumer goods and services. But it is a lie.

One of the reasons the message of advertising is a lie is that, while ads promise satisfaction, their purpose is to create dissatisfaction. Back in 1929 Floyd Allen, a motor industry executive, said, "Advertising is in the business of making people helpfully dissatisfied with what they have in favour of something better." We are like dogs chasing our tails, endlessly thinking that we could find true satisfaction if we could just own the latest gadget, the newest CD, or have a vacation. But each new thing leaves us wanting more. "He who loves money will not be satisfied with money, nor he who loves wealth with his income" (Eccles. 5:10).

Notice, too, the quasi-religious nature of these promises. The real issue is that consumerism is a false religion with false gods. Don Carson says: "In a former age, insatiable desire was understood to be a principal source of frustration, something to be opposed.

---

[14] Ibid.
[15] See http://www.adbusters.org.

Now it is to be cultivated as the engine that drives economic development. The endemic consumerism of the age feeds our greed, and even defines our humanity: we are not primarily worshipers, or thinkers, or God's image-bearers, or lovers, but consumers."[16] Material possessions do not bring contentment. A man's life does not consist in the abundance of his possessions.

The Good News of Christian Contentment

The lie of consumerism is a tyranny that enslaves us. While God rules through his Word, Satan rules through his lies—he is the father of lies. God's rule brings freedom. Satan's rule brings slavery. In his hymn "Lord, for the Years," Timothy Dudley-Smith speaks of our generation as "spirits oppressed by pleasure, wealth and care." This preoccupation with possessions is a form of oppression. It has been said that we work long hours to earn money to buy things we do not really need to impress people we do not really like. Meanwhile our families suffer. We do not have time to be human.

But the good news of the gospel is that we can be liberated from the lie of consumerism. For a time there was a "simple lifestyle" movement that advocated spending less and cutting out extravagance in our lives so we could give more. "Living simply that others might simply live" was one of its slogans. We have seen enough of the Bible's teaching on wealth and generosity to see the merit in this. But a challenge to give up is not enough to sustain us in a world heading in the opposite direction. We need a positive vision. The danger is that we degenerate into legalism, and legalism does not have the power to change lives. In Colossians Paul talks about people who set up rules: "Do not handle, Do not taste, Do not touch" (Col. 2:21), to which we might add, "Do not spend." "These have indeed an appearance of wisdom in promoting self-made religion and asceticism and severity to the body," Paul tells us. "But they are of no value in stopping the indulgence of the flesh" (Col. 2:23).

---

[16] D. A. Carson, *The Gagging of God: Christianity Confronts Pluralism* (Nottingham, UK: Apollos, 1996), 463.

Instead we need to proclaim the good news. We need gospel ethics. In a famous sermon entitled "The Expulsive Power of a New Affection," Thomas Chalmers, the nineteenth-century Scottish preacher, argued that we cannot simply tell ourselves to stop sinning. We need to direct the desires that sin falsely satisfies toward that which truly satisfies and liberates: God himself. If you told someone to destroy his house, Chalmers argues, then you might persuade him to do so reluctantly. But if you promised a far better house in its place, then he would destroy it gladly. It is the same with greed. Abstinence on its own is a hard road to follow. But the gospel promises true satisfaction and true joy. Sin involves living according to a lie, and we need to expose the lie of consumerism. But we need, too, to see the truth of the gospel and explore how we might live by that truth. We need to see how the gospel shows us a truer way and a better way. Mike Starkey says: "People in the West do "need" a lot of their consumer gimmickry to hold onto a sense of identity. The answer is less to tell people to throw away the trash than to teach people to root identity in more valuable sources, such as family, community, faith and a different set of values."[17]

When Paul writes to Timothy, telling him to stop certain false teachers in the churches in Ephesus, he reveals the true colors of these false teachers. They are lovers of money "who are depraved in mind and deprived of the truth, imagining that godliness is a means of gain" (1 Tim. 6:5). So Paul tells Timothy to teach and model a different lifestyle:

> But godliness with contentment is great gain, for we brought nothing into the world, and we cannot take anything out of the world. But if we have food and clothing, with these we will be content. But those who desire to be rich fall into temptation, into a snare, into many senseless and harmful desires that plunge people into ruin and destruction. For the love of money is a root of all kinds of evils. It is through this craving that some have wandered away from the faith and pierced themselves with many pangs.

---

[17] Starkey, *Born to Shop*, 59.

But as for you, O man of God, flee these things. Pursue righteousness, godliness, faith, love, steadfastness, gentleness. Fight the good fight of the faith. Take hold of the eternal life to which you were called and about which you made the good confession in the presence of many witnesses. I charge you in the presence of God, who gives life to all things, and of Christ Jesus, who in his testimony before Pontius Pilate made the good confession, to keep the commandment unstained and free from reproach until the appearing of our Lord Jesus Christ, which he will display at the proper time—he who is the blessed and only Sovereign, the King of kings and Lord of lords, who alone has immortality, who dwells in unapproachable light, whom no one has ever seen or can see. To him be honor and eternal dominion. Amen.

As for the rich in this present age, charge them not to be haughty, nor to set their hopes on the uncertainty of riches, but on God, who richly provides us with everything to enjoy. They are to do good, to be rich in good works, to be generous and ready to share, thus storing up treasure for themselves as a good foundation for the future, so that they may take hold of that which is truly life. (1 Tim. 6:6–19)

Contentment, says Paul, is "great gain" and urges us to be content with our food and clothing. Not only is contentment great gain but discontent is a sin. John Piper highlights the similarity between the first and last of the Ten Commandments: "You shall have no other gods before me" and "You shall not covet" (Ex. 20:3, 17). As John Piper explains, "Coveting is desiring anything other than God in a way that betrays a loss of contentment and satisfaction in him."[18] It is bad enough when rich Christians show little concern for the poor, but when they moan about their lot, they show contempt not only for the poor but also for the generosity of God. We have baptized the lie of consumerism and expect God to provide us with all that we want. At its most extreme this takes the form of the so-called prosperity gospel, which tells us that God will give us health and wealth if we just have enough faith

---

[18]John Piper, *Future Grace* (Colorado Springs, CO: Multnomah, 1995), 221.

in him. But the same attitude is apparent when we ask why God has allowed us to become unwell or not given us the new job we want. In 1 Corinthians 10 Paul warns his readers not to follow the example of the Israelites whom God rescued from Egypt: "And do not grumble, as some of them did—and were killed by the destroying angel." (1 Cor. 10:10 NIV). The psalmist says of them:

> Then they despised the pleasant land,
>   having no faith in his promise.
> They murmured in their tents,
>   and did not obey the voice of the LORD.
> Therefore he raised his hand and swore to them
>   that he would make them fall in the wilderness,
> and would make their offspring fall among the nations,
>   scattering them among the lands. (Ps. 106:24–27)

Paul could say: "I know how to be brought low, and I know how to abound. In any and every circumstance, I have learned the secret of facing plenty and hunger, abundance and need" (Phil. 4:12). Contentment can be learned. Indeed, contentment can be commanded (Luke 3:14; Heb. 13:5). So, what is the secret of contentment? First Timothy 6 gives us some clues.

1) Find Your Joy in God

The contentment that Paul describes as great gain comes together with godliness (1 Tim. 6:6). If, as Jesus says, "one's life does not consist in the abundance of his possessions" (Luke 12:15), then of what does it consist? The answer is that life consists in *relationships*. One of our problems is that we work our guts off to be well-off without ever really asking what "being well-off" really means. True life is found in relationships with our family, with our friends, with other people, with our neighbors, with people around the world, with creation, and ultimately with God himself. "And this is eternal life, that they know you the only true God, and Jesus Christ whom you have sent" (John 17:3). It is Jesus, not material possessions, that offers life to the full (John 10:10). John Piper says: "The fight of faith is the fight to keep your heart contented in Christ—to really believe, and keep on believing, that he will meet every need and satisfy every longing."[19] True life does not consist in what we own or what we possess. True life consists in knowing God. In Psalm 37 the psalmist says: "Delight yourself in the LORD, and he will give you the desires of your heart" (Ps. 37:4). The second half of the verse would sound like an exhortation to greed were it not for the fact the first half of the verse has redefined the desires of our heart. God promises to satisfy those who seek fulfilment and meaning in him.

There is an old adage that Christians do not tell lies—they sing them. Consider, then, the words of Graham Kendrick's song based on Philippians 3:

> All I once held dear, built my life upon,
> all this world reveres, and wars to own,
> all I once thought gain I have counted loss;
> spent and worthless now, compared to this:
> knowing you, Jesus, knowing you.

As we sing these words, do we truly count the home, the job, the car, the vacation, the sports gear, the designer labels, the hi-fi, the CDs, the videos, and the gadgets all worthless compared to knowing Christ? The joke is told of a wealthy man who when he dies wants to take his wealth with him. So he arrives at the pearly gates with two suitcases full of gold bars. Saint Peter tells him that luggage is not allowed, but the man pleads so earnestly that, after taking a look in the suitcases, Peter lets him in. As the man struggles in with his suitcases, one of the angels asks Peter what they contain. Looking bemused, Peter replies: "Paving slabs!" (see Rev. 21:21). It reminds just how "rubbish" are the things this world values "because of the surpassing worth of knowing Christ Jesus my Lord" (Phil. 3:8).

In 1 Timothy 6:9–10 Paul describes those whose desire to be rich has led them into ruin and destruction: "It is through this

---

[19] Ibid., 222.

craving that some have wandered away from the faith and pierced themselves with many pangs" (1 Tim. 6:10). So Paul exhorts Timothy to "flee these things. Pursue righteousness, godliness, faith, love, steadfastness, gentleness" (1 Tim. 6:11). True contentment is found in loving God and doing his will. In 1 Timothy 6:15–16 Paul breaks into praise. Worship refocuses our attention on what is worthy and away from what is worthless. When we worship God, we are not only affirming his worth; we are also reminding each other that he is *more* worthy and *more* precious than anything else.

2) Find Your Security in God

"Command those who are rich in this present world," Paul instructs Timothy, "not to be arrogant nor to put their hope in wealth, which is so uncertain, but to put their hope in God" (1 Tim. 6:17 NIV). The writer of Hebrews says: "Keep your life free from love of money, and be content with what you have, for he has said, 'I will never leave you nor forsake you.'" (Heb. 13:5). And when Paul famously says, "I can do all things through him who strengthens me" (Phil. 4:13), he is actually talking about learning to be content. One of the reasons we are not content is that we do not trust God. We look for security in our mortgages, our pensions, or our savings rather than finding security in God. It is a failure of faith. This is Jesus's argument in Luke 12:22–31. The reason we do not put first God's kingdom is that we are too busy running after all the things that the pagan world runs after (vv. 29–31). And the reason we run after these things is our "little faith" (v. 28). So Jesus says: "Do not be anxious about your life, what you will eat, nor about your body, what you will put on" (v. 22). He invites us to consider the ravens and the lilies. God feeds the ravens and clothes the lilies, so "how much more will he clothe you, O you of little faith!" (v. 28).

3) Enjoy God's Good Creation

God, says Paul, "richly provides us with everything to enjoy" (1 Tim. 6:17). Paul is writing in a context in which some people were advocating aestheticism—giving up pleasure because they thought that all that is bodily and sensual is evil. True spirituality, they claimed, was found in abstaining from marriage and certain foods. But Paul says that true spirituality includes the recognition that Christ was "manifested in the flesh." It was the Christ manifested in the flesh who was "vindicated by the Spirit" (1 Tim. 3:16). The incarnation affirms the goodness of creation, and to be spiritual is to affirm God's goodness in creation. God made this world, and, though we have messed it up, it is still a good world with pleasures that God has given for us to enjoy. Paul describes the call to abstain from sex and certain foods as the teachings of demons, adding, "for everything God created is good, and nothing is to be rejected if it is received with thanksgiving" (1 Tim. 4:1–4).

The tragic irony of consumerism is that the preoccupation with getting more spoils our enjoyment of what we have or what is free. Contentment is about enjoying what you have without wanting more all the time. In other words, contentment is found not by getting more but by wanting less. Or rather it is found by enjoying those things that are of true value. G. K. Chesterton said: "There are two ways to get enough: one is to accumulate more and more. The other is to desire less." My grandmother is one of the most contented people I know. It is not that she owns a lot, because she does not. She lives off state benefits in a typical "back-to-back" terraced house in which she has lived all her life. But she is rich because she has everything she wants.

Godly contentment is not about austerity or asceticism. It is about enjoyment. In practice this might mean cutting back on our working hours so we can spend more time hanging out with family and friends. It might mean spending less time shopping so we can enjoy our garden or the local countryside. It might mean spending less on ourselves and more on other people. It might mean moving to a smaller house to reduce our mortgage so we can work a four-day week and release time for gospel work. It might mean borrowing something from a friend or from a library rather than feeling the need to own it. It might mean spending less time thinking about the latest gadget we want and more time celebrating the love and beauty of God. It might mean sharing our home and our meals with people in need who will appreciate the company and the food. It might mean integrating celebration into our lives.

The point is that none of these choices involve giving anything up—or at least nothing of true value. Instead, they involve opting for something of greater value. They are all choices that will bring more satisfaction if we can only grasp what it is that truly satisfies. Tony Campolo says our society is like a shop that has been broken into. But the intruders have not stolen anything. They have simply switched all the price tags around. The things that do not really matter have large price tags while the things of true value are regarded as worthless.[20] I do not want to pretend that with a few judicious choices life can be easy; Jesus said that in this world we will have trouble (John 16:33). But we can be liberated from the empty way of life around us.

4) Live for God's New Creation

Paul instructs Timothy to command people to be rich—not rich with wealth but rich in good deeds: "Command them to do good, to be rich in good deeds, and to be generous and willing to share" (1 Tim. 6:18 NIV). Generosity breaks the power of money. Jesus said: "No servant can serve two masters, for either he will hate the one and love the other, or he will be devoted to the one and despise the other. You cannot serve God and money" (Luke 16:13). Giving is the way in which we affirm and confirm the lordship of God in our lives in place of the lordship of money. It is the way in which we reassert our control over money, liberating ourselves from its control over us. In a society where money is everything, giving is a powerfully subversive act. It is an act of defiance. Each time we give we are saying, "There are things more important to me than money." Tony Campolo says: "The good news is that you can be

---

[20] Cited in Starkey, *Born to Shop*, 16.

delivered from this insanity into a lifestyle of joy and celebration and that joy and celebration is in giving."[21]

By being generous and willing to share, says Paul, the rich "lay up treasure for themselves as a firm foundation for the coming age, so that they may take hold of the life that is truly life" (1 Tim. 6:19 NIV). Paul has said we are to enjoy God's good creation. Now he says we are to live for God's new creation. The treasure of this earth does not last. Moth and rust destroy, thieves break in and steal (Matt. 6:19). Pension plans come to nothing, stock markets crash, businesses go into receivership. And even when it lasts in this life, it does not prepare for the life to come (Luke 12:16–21). But Paul talks about "a firm foundation for the coming age." Jesus says: "Lay up for yourselves treasures in heaven" (Matt 6:20). Peter speaks of "an inheritance that is imperishable, undefiled, and unfading, kept in heaven for you" (1 Pet. 1:4). People often say of wealth: "You can't take it with you." But Paul claims that we can! We can lay up treasure for the coming age. But to take our wealth with us, we must first convert it into the currency of heaven. And the currency of heaven is love. So Paul invites us to "be generous and willing to share."

On Tuesday, January 3, 1956, Jim Elliot and four other missionaries landed on a small strip of land in the jungles of Ecuador.[22] It was a dangerous landing, and they could not all land at once. For years they had been dreaming of and planning for this moment. Their hearts were set on reaching the Auca Indians with the good news of Jesus. The Aucas were a notoriously dangerous tribe. No one had reached them before. Some had exchanged gifts, but always the Aucas had attacked them. For three months the missionaries had been regularly flying over the area, dropping gifts and shouting greetings. When they landed they built a hut and waited for the Aucas to come and find them. They knew the dangers. Their wives had discussed the possibility of becoming

---

[21] Tony Campolo, *The Tourist Attraction* (London: Tearfund Video).
[22] Their story is told in Elisabeth Elliot, *Through Gates of Splendour* (London: Hodder & Stoughton, 1957).

widows. Elisabeth Elliot, the wife of Jim Elliot, says they went simply because they knew they belonged to God, because he was their creator and their redeemer. They had no choice but to willingly obey him, and that meant obeying his command to take the good news to every nation. On Friday, January 6, three Aucas—one man and two women—approached them. They exchanged greetings. The missionaries showed them rubber bands, yo-yos, and balloons, and the man was taken up in the plane.

On Sunday, January 8, they were due to radio in at 4:30. There was silence. When no message came, a plane was sent and then a rescue party. Four of their bodies were recovered—all lanced to death. The fifth was never found. It seems they were ambushed. All five were martyred for the sake of Christ. All were married, and four were fathers. One wife was pregnant. Her three-year-old was heard to tell the new crying baby, "Never you mind, when we get to heaven I'll show you which one is daddy." Jim Elliot once said: "He is no fool who gives what he cannot keep to gain what he cannot lose." Jim Elliot had seen through the lie of consumerism. He had seen the emptiness of all this world offers. He had realized the far greater value of the new creation that God promises.

I have a friend who is an octogenarian. He was telling me how, as he regularly walks along the River Thames, he has often got into conversation with a man tending his garden in one of the big houses by the river. One day the man said, "Do you know who I am?" It turned out he was the owner of a chain of local garden centers. "I'm worth 4 million pounds," he said. But then he added: "But I"m ninety-three, and soon I'll be gone, and what will it be worth to me then?" And my friend told me he walked away thinking, "I am far richer than this poor man."

Jim Elliot's diary was found by the rescue party. These were the last words he wrote as they waited for the Aucas Indians to come to them:

> I walked out to the hill just now. It is exalting, delicious, to stand
> embraced by the shadows of a friendly tree with the wind tug-

ging at your coattail and the heavens hailing your heart, to gaze
and glory and give oneself again to God—what more could a man
ask? Oh, the fullness, pleasure, sheer excitement of knowing God
on earth! I care not if I never raise my voice again for him, if only
I may love him, please him. Perhaps in mercy he shall give me
a host of children [i.e., converts] that I may lead them through
the vast star fields to explore his delicacies whose finger ends set
them to burning. But if not, if only I may see him, touch his gar-
ments, and smile into his eyes—ah then, not stars nor children
shall matter, only himself.

O Jesus, Master and Centre and End of all, how long before
that glory is yours which has so long awaited you? Now there is
no thought of you among men; then there shall be thought for
nothing else. Now other men are praised; then none shall care
for any other's merits. Hasten, hasten, Glory of Heaven, take your
crown, subdue your kingdom, enthrall your creatures.[23]

Paul says that by being generous and willing to share we can
"take hold of that which is truly life" 1 Tim. 6:19). It is a wonderful
statement. The good news of the gospel is that there is an alternative to the empty way of life offered by consumerism. We can
enjoy the life that is truly life.

A Gospel-Centered Life

Tom Sine talks about discipleship as a three-legged stool. Evangelicals have been good at two of the legs: spiritual transformation
(things like reading the Bible and prayer) and moral transformation (things like sexual purity and moral integrity). But we have
neglected the third leg of cultural transformation—having biblical values instead of worldly values. Let me illustrate. If someone
in your congregation said he was having an affair, you would be
rightly horrified. If someone in your congregation said she was
going for a better-paying job, we might well commend her, even
if she did not really need a higher salary. But alongside his call
to put to death sexual immortality, Paul says we must also put to

---

[23] Elisabeth Elliot, *Through Gates of Splendour* (London: Hodder & Stoughton, 1957), 256.

death "greed, which is idolatry" (Col. 3:5 NIV). Don Carson says: "There are Christians who formally espouse the historic faith but whose heartbeat is for more and more of this world's goods, whose dreams are not for heaven and for the glory of God, but for success, financial independence, a bigger house, a finer car."[24]

Many Christians make life choices by deciding first on the lifestyle to be adopted, and then they choose a job to fund that lifestyle, then a home nearby before finally choosing a local church. In fact, the first element—the lifestyle—is often not a conscious decision at all. Rather, our assumptions about an appropriate lifestyle are shaped by the values of the world around us. So we pursue a lifestyle that is pretty much like everyone else's. We live in the same sort of places, enjoy the same sort of vacations, drive the same sort of cars, and so on. Even if we cannot afford the full package, it is what we aspire to. We worry about young people in our churches being corrupted by the values of the world, but Jim Wallis points out the real problem is not that they have failed to learn our values. The real problem is that they have. "They can see beneath our social and religious platitudes to what we care about most. Our great cultural message comes through loud and clear: it is an affluent lifestyle that counts for success and happiness."[25]

So to live that lifestyle that we aspire to, we look for a job that will earn enough to pay for it. We assume we should try to get on in our careers, even making a virtue out of it. With the job in place we look for a home nearby; then we look for a church and perhaps volunteer for some aspect of Christian ministry in our spare time. We might call this *leftover discipleship*. My commitment to the church and to Christian service comes from the leftovers of my life. And my giving is from the leftovers of my money.

There is an alternative model, one which challenges this model at two levels. First, we need to be intentional about our lifestyles. Instead of uncritically adopting the values of the Western dream, we need to shape our lives around a biblical vision of the good

---

[24] Carson, *The Gagging of God*, 465.
[25] Jim Wallis, *The Soul of Politics* (New York: Fount, 1994), 137.

life. Second, we need to be more intentional about our lives and ministries. If we adopted this alternative model, our first decisions in life would not be about lifestyle and job but about church and ministry. We would begin with a commitment to seek first God's kingdom. We would see ourselves first and foremost as gospel ministers and members of gospel communities. We would consider the gifts and passions God has given us. We could consider the needs of our church and local communities. We would decide first what our ministry is going to be. It might be sharing the gospel with elderly people or caring for the homeless or bringing Christian values to the business world or providing pastoral care in the church. It could be any one of a hundred things. Then we would look for a home near our ministries and churches. It may involve relocating to serve the needs of a local neighborhood or to be close to a particular Christian community. Only then would we make decisions about a job, and that choice would be determined by what enabled us to do our ministries.

Some might pursue a ministry through their career, but they will be intentional about that, seeing it as their ministry and not an end in itself. What would count would no longer be the Western dream but serving God and putting first his kingdom. Instead of leftover service, we would have whole-life discipleship and left-over lifestyles. We would be content with whatever standard of living allowed us to serve God and seek first his kingdom.

This model is *not* far-fetched. I know plenty of people who have done it. Whereas most of us try to fit serving God around the edges of our lives, they are seeking first the kingdom of God. I know a married couple in which the husband is a judge, the wife spends her life coordinating mission links, and their beautiful home is frequently full of young people. I once heard of a man who earned £140,000 a year. He and his family live on £40,000 so he can give £100,000 away. A group of young men pledged to work no more than 25 hours a week for money so that they have significant time to work with children at risk, even though this means they have had to reduce their standard of living. Some of us may have to remake decisions and unpick past decisions. There is a sense in which instead of a thousand dilemmas about how we should use our money, we have to make one fundamental choice: do we live for God or for money? It is because we waver about this decision that we replicate it day by day. "No one can serve two masters, for either he will hate the one and love the other, or he will be devoted to the one and despise the other. You cannot serve God and money (Matt. 6:24).

Summary

Many people live their lives according to the lie of consumerism, that we can find identity and fulfillment through consumer goods. But the gospel liberates us from this lie to find joy in knowing and serving God.

We have looked at the case for social involvement, how it relates to evangelism and to the content of the gospel. The next three chapters consider something of the *how* of social involvement. We begin by exploring the nature of poverty.

Welcoming the
Excluded

Over one billion people live on less than one dollar a day, with nearly half the world's population—2.8 billion people—surviving on less than two dollars.[1] The numbers of people in extreme poverty are greatest in South Asia, while the proportion is highest in sub-Saharan Africa. More than 800 million people go to bed hungry every day, 300 million of whom are children. Every year six million children die from malnutrition before they reach their fifth birthday. Around 114 million children receive no formal education, and 584 million women are illiterate. Every thirty seconds an African child dies of malaria. Every day HIV/AIDS kills six thousand people, while another 8,200 people are infected with the virus. More than 2.6 billion people—about 40 percent of the world's population—do not have basic sanitations, and one billion use unsafe sources of drinking water. Four out of every ten people do not have access to even a simple latrine.[2]

Meanwhile the world's 497 billionaires have more than twice as much financial wealth as the 2.4 billion people living in low-income countries.[3] What the United States spends on cosmetics would pro-

---

[1] http://www.guardian.co.uk/politics/2005/may/15/uk.g81.
[2] Figures from the United Nations Millennium Project, http://www.unmillenniumproject.org/documents/3-MP-PovertyFacts-E.pdf.
[3] http://www.globalissues.org/article/26/poverty-facts-and-stats.

vide basic education for all. What Europe spends on ice cream would provide water and sanitation for all. Providing basic health and nutrition for all would cost $13 billion according to the United Nations Development Programme (UNDP). Europe and the United States spend £17 billion on pet foods each year. Each year Europe spends $50 billion on cigarettes and $105 billion on alcoholic drinks. Military spending around the world is $780 billion each year.[4]

To put these statistics into some sort of perspective, consider what the world would look like if it were reduced to one village of one hundred people. Twenty of the villagers would have over three-quarters of the wealth, while twenty of the villagers would be left with just 1.5 percent of the wealth. Sixteen would be unable to read, and eleven would go to bed hungry each day. Fourteen would be unable to drink clean water, and forty would have inadequate sanitation. Seventeen of the women would have experienced some form of domestic violence in their lives. Half the village would be living on less than two dollars a day—that's at least one of your neighbors.

It is not all bad news. The number of people living under the international poverty line of $1.25 a day declined from 1.8 billion to 1.4 billion between 1900 and 2005, while the proportion of people living in extreme poverty in developing regions dropped from 46 percent to 27 percent.[5] Enrollment in primary education in developing regions reached 89 percent in 2008, up from 83 percent in 2000.[6] The number of children in developing countries who die before they reach the age of five has dropped from one hundred out of every one thousand live births in 1990 to seventy-two in 2008.[7] The number of women dying in childbirth has almost halved over the last twenty years.[8] Around 1.7 billion people have gained access to safe drinking water since 1990.[9]

---

[4] United Nations Human Development Report 1998, p. 37, http://hdr.undp.org/en/reports/global/hdr1998.
[5] http://www.un.org/millenniumgoals/pdf/MDG_FS_1_EN.pdf.
[6] http://www.un.org/millenniumgoals/pdf/MDG_FS_2_EN.pdf.
[7] http://www.un.org/millenniumgoals/pdf/MDG_FS_4_EN.pdf.
[8] http://www.un.org/apps/news/story.asp?NewsID=42013&Cr=maternal&Crl=.
[9] http://www.un.org/millenniumgoals/pdf/MDG_FS_7_EN.pdf.

People have always talked about poverty. It has a rich vocabulary in most cultures. One of the first empirical studies was that of William Booth, the founder of the Salvation Army. His book *In Darkest England* (1890) exposed the plight of London's poor. In 1901 Benjamin Rowntree, a member of the Quaker chocolate-manufacturing family, published *Poverty: A Study of Town Life*. This study of poverty in York was one of the first attempts to develop a measure of poverty. Rowntree used a standard based on a family's ability to meet four basic requirements: food, fuel, shelter, and clothing. By the 1960s the main focus was on levels of income, reflected in indicators like gross national product (GNP) per person. The problem with GNP as a measure is that it measures only economic activity, so crime adds to GNP (since it requires more lawyers, police, and prisons) as do cigarette addiction and arms expenditure. Voluntary work and unpaid household work are excluded, while the exploitation of natural resources is included as a benefit, not as a cost.

Analysts realized that economic indicators were an inadequate definition of well-being and poverty, and other measures were needed. The UNDP has tried to overcome some of these problems by developing the "Human Development Index," which combines measures of health, education, and income. During the 1970s there was a growing emphasis on relative poverty. Poverty is not just about not having enough; it is also about inequality and being unable to join in with your community. In the 1980s Robert Chambers and others highlighted the importance of vulnerability and insecurity in shaping people's experience of poverty. People move in and out of poverty over time. So along with low income it is important to consider their ability to cope with problems. If they do not have savings or a network of relationships, a crisis may tip them into poverty. In the 1990s these insights came together in the notion of "social exclusion." This saw poverty in relational terms as the inability to benefit from democratic and legal systems, markets, welfare state provisions, and family and community. Increasingly people have realized that, while income is a central element in poverty, poverty is as much about powerlessness and marginalization.

The most commonly used word for "the poor" in the Old Testament has the sense of "weak, miserable, helpless and suffering."[10] But because it implies dependence on others, it is also used figuratively in the Psalms to describe the petitioner's position before God. Likewise, the most common word in the New Testament means in classical Greek "poor like a beggar," but its use is colored by the Old Testament vocabulary so that it can be used both of the economically destitute and the spiritually humble. Indeed, spiritual and economic poverty are often linked when through persecution the faithful are reduced to poverty or when the socially poor turn to God as their only hope. In James 2:5 spiritual wealth is attributed to the faithful who are economically poor: "Has not God chosen those who are poor in the world to be rich in faith and heirs of the kingdom, which he has promised to those who love him?" (James 2:5).

Notice the language James uses to describe the poor: "Religion that is pure and undefiled before God, the Father, is this: to visit orphans and widows in their affliction" (James 1:27). But James is interested not only in widows and orphans; he is concerned about other needy people as well. James is using widows and orphans to describe all those who are vulnerable because of their marginalized status. In doing so James is picking up the language of the Old Testament. Widows, orphans, and aliens (immigrants) are often used in the Old Testament to describe all those in poverty. God himself "watches over the sojourners; he upholds the widow and the fatherless" (Ps. 146:9). Joel Green explains how in Jesus's time "poor" was a term for "those of low status, for those excluded from the normal canons of status honour." This low

---

[10] H. Kvalbein, "Poor/Poverty," *New Dictionary of Biblical Theology* (Nottingham, UK: Inter-Varsity, 2000), 687–91; W. R. Domeris, "ebyôn," *New International Dictionary of Old Testament Theology and Exegesis*, vol. 1 (Carlisle, UK: Paternoster, 1997), 228–32; W. J. Drumbrell, "ānāw," *New International Dictionary of Old Testament Theology and Exegesis*, vol. 3 (Carlisle, UK: Paternoster, 1997), 454–64; and L. Coenen, C. Brown, and H. –H. Esser, "Poor," *New International Dictionary of New Testament Theology*, rev. ed. (Carlisle, UK: Paternoster, 1971, 1986), 82029.

status might arise because of economic disadvantage, but status was also defined by "education, gender, family heritage, religious purity, vocation, economics and so on."[11] The poor are those of low status, the excluded.

Stan and Mari Thekaekara work with tribal peoples in the Nilgiris Hills of India. Their reflections on visiting a number of projects in inner-city areas of the United Kingdom are reproduced in a report from the Centre for Innovation in Voluntary Action:

> On arriving in the UK, it is difficult at first for a visitor from a Third World country to immediately perceive that poverty exists at all. Everyone was better housed, clad and fed. Everyone seemed to have a television, a fridge—some even had cars—all items of luxury for the majority of people in India. But as the week went by we began to see beyond the televisions, refrigerators and cars. Amazingly, similarities between the people of Easterhouse and the Paniyas of the Nilgiris began to emerge. Though the face of poverty was completely different, the impact was exactly the same.[12]

Poverty is about the lack of income and resources, both an absolute lack and a relative lack. But these things are symptoms of underlying issues. At root, poverty is about broken relationships—relationships with God, within and between communities, and with the environment. Poverty is social as well as economic. God made us as stewards of creation to contribute to community life, but the poor become noncontributors. They are forced to be passive. The result is a loss of dignity, confidence, and hope that in turn become significant factors keeping them in poverty. So poverty is about marginalization, vulnerability, isolation, and exclusion. And so the Bible refers to the widow and orphan to represent those who are vulnerable because of their marginalized status.

A relational approach to poverty also enables us to recognize the poverty of the economically rich. The economically rich can

[11]Joel Green, *The Gospel of Luke*, New International Commentary on the New Testament (Grand Rapids, MI: Eerdmans, 1997), 211.
[12]Cited in Ingrid Hanson, *Faces of Poverty: The States of Britain in the 90s* (London: Tearfund, 1996).

be relationally poor. Indeed, when one remembers that the most enriching relationship is our relationship with God, the rich for whom it is so hard to enter the kingdom of God are often the most spiritually impoverished. In contrast, James asks, "Has not God choosen those who are poor in the world to be rich in faith and heirs of the kingdom, which he has promised to those who love him?" (James 2:5). When I was a child our family had a low income. We received free school meals from the government and never had the toys and vacations that other children had. But I never felt poor. I was part of a loving family, receiving a good education, and part of a network of supportive relationships. I did not feel vulnerable, nor did I feel as if I lacked choices. It was only as I looked back that I realized we were economically poor. At the time I did not perceive this, because we were emotionally and relationally rich.

The Poverty Web

Poverty is rarely the result of one cause. There may be one present-ing issue or an immediate cause of poverty, but this will rarely be the only factor. Poverty involves a cocktail of issues. In his book *Rural Development: Putting the Last First*, Robert Chambers outlines a web of interlocking factors that bind people in poverty:[13]

1) *Lack of resources.* Poor income or lack of capital means people cannot provide for their needs or protect against crises.
2) *Physical weakness.* Illness, handicap, and weakness reduce peo-ple's employability or productivity and increase their social exclusion.
3) *Isolation.* Marginalization is a defining characteristic of poverty, whether it is the result of geographic isolation, poor education, or cultural attitudes to race, gender, or diseases like HIV/AIDS.
4) *Powerlessness.* When people lack effective access to political or judicial processes, they are vulnerable to exploitation and corruption.

---

[13] Robert Chambers, *Rural Development: Putting the Last First* (London: Longman, 1983), 103–39.

5) *Vulnerability*. Natural disasters and family crises only cause poverty when individuals and communities are already vulnerable through social marginalization and inadequate assets.

I want to add a couple of factors to Chambers's model:

6) *Cultural attitudes and expectations.* Chambers's postmodernism makes him reluctant to criticize another person's worldview, but cultural attitudes, such as those toward women, can reinforce the marginalization of the poor, and factors such as dowry expectations or extravagant wedding celebrations can exacerbate vulnerabilities.

7) *Hopelessness and demotivation.* Poverty destroys your motivation and hope. You are knocked back so many times you stop trying. You are not prepared to be humiliated again. In a similar way, under dictatorships you survive by keeping your head down and learn to avoid taking initiatives. Reflecting on the impediments to development in post–Khmer Rouge Cambodia, Meas Nee, a Khmer said: "You cannot easily change the damage caused by the war, or caused by the systematic breaking of relationships, or the loss of dignity. You cannot easily change the damage done by the meetings held in fear, or the meetings at which people were harangued by propaganda. The mind is paralysed by such things so the way forward is slowly, carefully."[14]

Moreover, these community-level factors operate within a broader social, economic, and political environment:

1) *Weak social capital.* The cohesion and connectedness within communities and societies create opportunities to escape poverty and reduce the vulnerability of the poor. When there is no one to turn to for a loan, a job reference, advice, or help in a crisis, you are much more likely to remain in poverty.

2) *Weak civil society.* Healthy civil society groups, such as churches, trade unions and cooperatives, as well as social clubs foster a

---

[14] Sheila Melot, *Getting People Thinking* (London: Tearfund Case Studies), http://tilz.tearfund.org /webdocs/Tilz/Roots/GPTENG_full%20doc.pdf.

democratic culture and act as a bulwark against the power of the state and the market. Where these are absent or weak, people lack opportunities for participation in their communities.

3) *Corruption and a lack of accountability.* A lack of institutional and political accountability leads to the corruption that excludes those without money or social capital from services and the processes of justice.

4) *Economic mismanagement.* Poor or unjust national and international policies that impede economic growth or deny access to international markets prevent the poor having access to resources and market opportunities.

5) *Poor governance.* Inefficient bureaucracies, a breakdown of the rule of law, undemocratic systems, and a lack of commitment to human rights all increase the powerlessness and marginalization of the poor.

These local, national, and international factors together represent the causes of poverty, and to a certain extent they define what poverty is. Moreover, the components of this poverty web rarely work in isolation. They reinforce one another, creating a ratchet that locks people in poverty. Addressing just one factor will rarely be effective if other factors are left unaddressed. This means that social involvement cannot tackle the symptoms of poverty in isolation. Drilling a well in a village may provide clean water, but it will not overcome poverty if other causes and symptoms of poverty are not addressed. If the marginalization of certain groups within the community is not addressed, then they may be excluded from the benefits the well brings. If a fatalistic worldview is not challenged, then the well may be underused. If the community is not mobilized, then it may not cope if the water pump breaks down. In the same way, research shows that health programs have little effect if they are not integrated with a concern for the wider factors that cause ill health, like underemployment, inadequate sanitation, and poor housing. Development must not simply address the needs of individuals and households. Individuals are part of communities, and their needs are enmeshed with the needs of the community. The well-being of the community as a whole affects households within it.

Poverty and Sin

It is, of course, a truism to say that poverty is the result of sin. In helping people think about the underlying causes of poverty, I have sometimes used a "spider's web" analysis. We write a symptom of poverty in the center of a large piece of paper and keep asking, "Why?" The question "Why does a child die of diarrhea?" will throw up a number of answers: poor hygiene, inadequate sanitation, no local health services, and so on. Then to each of these we ask, "Why?" This throws up another layer of answers to which we again ask, "Why?" This creates an expanding and interlocking web of factors. I have a copy of a spider's web analysis that was done by a group in Bangladesh. What is striking about it is that, more than once, at its outer reaches are "Adam and Eve." This group linked poverty back to humanity's fall into sin. Why does Abdul have diarrhea? Because he drinks sugar water. Why does he drink sugar water? Because it is advertised, because big companies want to profit from the poor, because of greed, because of Adam and Eve. Or again: Why does Abdul have diarrhea? Because he has measles. Why does he have measles? Because he has not been vaccinated, because vaccines are not available, because of the misappropriation of public funds, because of dishonesty, because of low spiritual and moral values, because of Adam and Eve.

It is the fundamental characteristic of sin that we want to be god of our own lives. In the garden we rejected the life that God had given us. We chose to live for ourselves. We chose to be gods over our own lives. This means that when we interact with each other, our interaction is characterized by competition and conflict. I will not let you be god over my life but will try to impose my will over you. Jayakumar Christian, an Indian development practitioner with World Vision, talks of the "the god-complexes" of the rich.[15]

---

[15] Bryant Myers, *Walking with the Poor* (Maryknoll: Orbis, 1999), 14–15, 72–80.

The rich create stories and systems that justify their privileged position, and the poor begin to internalize these, thinking of them as normal.

Sin is relational. It begins with the rejection of God as God in our lives. It is the rejection of his love. This broken relationship leads to broken relationships between human beings. Adam and Eve shift the blame from one to the other. Now the woman will be oppressed by the man. Cain kills Abel. And it leads to a broken relationship between humanity and creation. Now agriculture will be characterized by frustration and toil. It is this relational breakdown that underlies the reality of poverty. Poverty is more than the absence of income, resources, or skills. It is about powerlessness, isolation, exclusion, and marginalization—all relational terms. Poverty stems from the broken relationships between God and mankind, within communities and between communities, and between mankind and the environment.

In summary, poverty is social as well as economic. It is not simply the lack, or relative lack, of income. It is about marginalization, vulnerability, isolation, and exclusion. This is consistent with the biblical emphasis on the "widow" and "orphan" representing those who are vulnerable because of their marginalized status. Poverty is relational and stems from the broken relationships between God and humanity.

Social Involvement and the Church

Recognizing that poverty is about marginalization and exclusion presents a clear opportunity for the church. At a poverty hearing organized by Church Action on Poverty, Mrs. Jones, a mother who has lived in poverty all her life, described the experience of poverty like this: "In part it is about having no money, but there is more to poverty than that. It is about being isolated, unsupported, uneducated and unwanted. Poor people want to be included and not just judged and 'rescued' at times of crisis."[16] So the first re-

---

[16] Cited in Paul Vallely, "Mrs. Jones Has Something to Say," *The Independent* (August 7, 1996).

sponsibility of the church in terms of social involvement is to be a community of love and inclusion—to be the church. We are to offer welcome and belonging to people, especially people who are marginalized by society.

Jesus made a point of including the marginalized and sinners. The religious people of his day despised him for it. In Luke 7 Jesus says the religious leaders are like children who cannot be pleased. They complained that John the Baptist fasted too much. Now they complain that Jesus feasts too much. The Son of Man has come eating and drinking, and you say, 'Look at him! A glutton and a drunkard, a friend of tax collectors and sinners!'" (v. 34). The Son of Man is a reference to the one who comes in glory to rule all things (see Dan. 7:13–14). But "the Son of Man has come eating and drinking." It echoes Isaiah 25:6–8 and 55:1–2 in which Isaiah describes God's promised future as a great feast of provision and enjoyment, acceptance and friendship. The religious leaders have no problem with this. They do not take exception to the coming of God's messianic feast; that was what they longed for. What they object to is the invitation list. Jesus feasts with the wrong sort of people. In Jesus's day eating with someone was a sign of acceptance and inclusion. This is why Jesus got into such trouble when he partied with the socially marginalized of his day. By eating with "sinners" Jesus modeled the radical grace of God. In response to the accusation that Jesus is "a glutton and a drunkard, and a friend of the worst sort of sinners" (Luke 7:34), Luke tells a story that shows that the accusation is true (7:36–50)! He shows that Jesus *does* feast and drink and that he is a friend of the worst sort of sinners.

It is striking that in the New Testament there is no talk of social projects, nor for that matter is there much on evangelistic methods. Instead the New Testament talks about the church being the church: a caring, gracious, and inclusive community with a message to proclaim. We are to include the poor in the network of believing relationships. In this way we offer them dignity, belonging, and inclusion. They are no longer isolated but people with connections and people with a contribution to make. I remember a woman with an alcoholic husband and two disruptive children. What she liked about coming to our church was that we did not "tut tut" when her children acted up. We welcomed her and her children along with the disruption they brought. It was decisive in her Christian experience. Many people suggest that the main factors behind the phenomenal growth of Pentecostalism among the poor of the world is that their approach to spiritual gifts and ministry means everyone's contribution is valued irrespective of education, status, and wealth. In other denominations the clergy perform the religious activities. In Pentecostalism anyone can speak the Word of God to the congregation. They offer a sense of family and the support of family to people displaced and disoriented by a move to the city or by the complexity of modern life.

The church has often had a presence in a local community for years. That means both that it is well placed to work with the poor, but also that its work is likely to be sustainable in the long term. As Gladys Wathanga, a Tearfund worker, says: "I know that when I go back to Kenya my church will still be there, but I don't know whether my development organization will be. They are in today and could be out tomorrow, but the local church is there for years."[17] Sustainable Christian development requires sustainable Christian communities. In other words, while it is possible to have sustainable development without local churches, you cannot have sustainable *Christian* development—development that is distinctly Christian—without sustainable Christian communities. This means that Christian development must be accompanied by church planting where no churches exist.

Perhaps the most powerful tool in Christian social involvement, a tool with the potential to make a huge impact on our communities, is the humble teapot. Let me explain. Within a short walk of the average town church in the United States there are likely to be ten thousand people, including something like:

---

[17]Cited in Tulo Raistrick and Tim Chester, "The Church and Its Role in Development," unpublished paper, 1999.

- 2,700 people living alone
- 74 people who have been divorced within the last year
- 356 single parents
- 343 pregnant teenagers
- 39 recent abortions
- 1,658 people who are unemployed
- 1,170 people living in poverty
- 414 people with a seriously debilitating mental illness
- 1,508 bereavements within the last year
- 473 people living in households without a car
- 45 people in a nursing home
- 2,900 people serving as family caregivers for an ill or disabled relative
- 112 homeless people in temporary accommodation
- two asylum seekers[18]

The striking thing about these statistics is how many of these problems can be met in some measure by simple human contact. It can simply involve sharing a cup of tea. A Christian friend of mine was talking with a social worker in a poor area of London. This social worker is a Marxist, so he has no particular sympathy for Christianity. My friend asked him whether the church made much of an impact in the community in which he worked. The social worker said: "If you mean the public face of the church—its pronouncement, its projects, and its initiatives—then the answer is resoundingly no. But if you took away all the kindnesses and neighborly acts that Christians do—visiting the sick, shopping for the housebound, and so on—then this community would fall apart." Community involvement need not involve big projects with local authority funding. What counts is ordinary Christians with commitment and compassion.

El Retono is a rehab house for drug addicts from the slums of Buenos Aires, Argentina. They have some small businesses in

---

[18] Figures based on statistics from http://www.census.gov plus www.cdc.gov/nchs/fastats/teen birth; http://www.dhs.gov/xlibrary/assets/statistics/publications.ois_rfa_fr_2010, http://www.nationalhomeless.org/factsheets/How_many; http://www.disastercenter.com/crime/uscrime.htm; and http://www.caregiving.org/data/Caregiving_in_the_US_2009_full_report.pdf.

which the men work, and they provide therapy sessions. The set-up is simple and plain. El Retono is aimed at the poorer section of the community, which cannot pay for rehab. The church pays the salary of Kike, the head of El Retono. But the living expenses of the men come from the income they earn together. Sometimes there is no food, although when I visited we all had a big plate of rice with a piece of steak on top! El Retono has four planks to its work: work, therapy, living as a community, and church. Attendance at church is an integral part of the program. This can be hard work for both members of El Retono and members of the church, but crucial. Kike told me that the link with the local church was an essential part of the success of their work. This is because the church provides an intermediate community in which people learn social skills and gain confidence. Plus the gospel is proclaimed and lived by the church. Kike is himself a former drug addict. He linked up with the church, he told me, to exploit their generosity. But through their unwavering commitment to him, he became a Christian.

We are not simply talking about inviting the poor to come to church on Sunday mornings. Often there is a significant gap between the church and outsiders and between the culture of the church and the culture of the marginalized. I have friends who began working with a local church in a poor area of Mexico City. The members of the church were more affluent and came from outside the area in which the church building was located. The church wanted to reach people from the local area and initially welcomed the help they received. The couple began to reach prostitutes and drug addicts, befriending them, ministering to their needs, and sharing the gospel with them. Much of the work was funded with their own money. They started to see some of the prostitutes and drug addicts coming to the meetings of the church. The couple were excited about the ways things were developing and the opportunities that were opening up to reach marginalized people. But one Sunday morning they turned up to find the building locked. The members of the church felt they did not want prostitutes and drug addicts corrupting their children. They had decided to move elsewhere without telling the couple. The ministry collapsed overnight. The culture gap between the church and the marginalized had proved too big for the church members.

I once asked the members of my church to go into a betting shop and place a bet on a horse before the next meeting.[19] About half of them did it, myself included. The following week I asked people what it felt like. This is a selection of our replies:

- It was an alien environment.
- I hadn't got a clue what to do.
- It was better with a friend.
- I felt very awkward, nervous, very odd and on edge.
- I felt that people were looking at me.
- No one talked to me, and I was glad about that.
- I wanted to get in and out as quickly as possible.
- The people inside were very different from me.

The excuses of those who did not do it were just as revealing:

- I don't agree with it.
- I didn't want to be seen.
- I didn't want to be misinterpreted.
- I couldn't be bothered.
- I was brought up a Methodist.
- I wouldn't know what to do.
- I would be excruciatingly embarrassed.
- I wouldn't like the people in there.

This is how most people today feel about going to church. A lot of evangelism revolves around getting people to come to church or church events. For some this is appropriate, but most people are no more likely to enter a church than you or I are to go into a betting shop. If we are going to offer a place of inclusion to the poor, then we have to make the Christian community one of welcome and

---

[19] Based on an exercise in Tulo Raistrick, *Church, Community and Change: The Manual*, Part 1 (London: Tearfund, 2000), 51–53.

belonging. Church is where we feel safe and comfortable. Church is where non-Christians feel embarrassed and awkward. We need to take the gospel and the church out of our ghetto and into the world around us. The inclusion of the Christian community does not have to take place in a church building. It is about relationships, not institutions. A house group may be a place to begin.

A minister in Scotland was once standing outside his church when a drunk walked past. "Why don't you come in?" he asked. "I will," said the drunk, "when I get my life sorted out." The minister was quick-witted enough to question whether this was likely. But he was left with a more fundamental question: "Whoever gave him the impression that church was for people who had got their lives sorted out?" To be a place of welcome for the marginalized we will have to be honest about our own brokenness. And even more importantly, we need to be communities of grace. My life may be more sorted out than someone else's, but that is not a testament to my effort or initiative. It is a testament to God's grace, perhaps over years and even over generations. It is only by celebrating grace, proclaiming grace, and living by grace that we will attract marginalized sinners as Jesus did (Luke 15:1–2).

The Valley of Praise

I was telling one of my colleagues that my vision for Christian mission and social involvement was neither sophisticated evangelistic programs nor professional development projects, but for small, inclusive, caring communities of believers. And he embodied that for me as he told me of a church he had visited in the slums of Bombay called "The Valley of Praise." The leaders live in a ground-floor room, and the church meets in the room above. They have an AIDS clinic in a room across the passage. The upper room in which the congregation meets is also used for preschool classes, overnight accommodation for street children, the clinic, and a small library of literature. This, it seems to me, corresponds to the New Testament vision of both evangelism and social involvement.

This is the vehicle for Christian hope in our world. The kingdom of God has not been given to those who wield political influence or who run national evangelistic campaigns or who receive media attention. The kingdom of God has been given to Christ's "little flock" (Luke 12:32).

Summary

Poverty is about marginalization, vulnerability, isolation, and exclusion. One of the most important things that the church can do for the poor is to be the church, to be a place where people find welcome and belonging.

9

Strengthening the Powerless

I remember helping a refugee move into a new flat that had been provided for him by a housing association with the help of a Christian friend. While I cleaned the kitchen, I heard the Christian friend making a list of the things our refugee friend needed. Every now and then my Christian friend would ask me what I thought. And every now and then our refugee friend protested at something on the list or the need to produce a list at all. In the end I intervened: "Don't try to manage his life." Our Afghan friend had poor English and did not understand the system. He needed help. He needed help understanding the decisions that faced him and how he might implement them. He was not going to be helped by someone making those decisions for him. It is a big temptation for us to take over the lives of the poor. But we must serve the poor, not run their lives for them. As always, the cross is our model: "The Son of Man came not to be served but to serve, and to give his life as a ransom for many" (Mark 10:45).

In the last chapter we saw that poverty was about marginalization and powerlessness. Poverty as marginalization means that the first responsibility of the church in relation to social involvement is to be the church, a place of welcome and inclusion. Poverty as powerlessness means that social involvement should be about strengthening the weak. Consider the following quotes from

Moraene Roberts, unemployed and registered disabled, speaking to church and political leaders at a National Poverty Hearing:

> We are judged by people who have no understanding of the pressures of our lives. The authorities feel they can impose their own agenda on us.
>
> No-one asks our views. We see many millions of pounds wasted in inappropriate initiatives based on the very expensive advice of academic experts who have never lived in poverty. But we are the real experts of our own hopes and aspirations. Service providers should ask the users before deciding on policies, before setting targets that will affect our lives. We can contribute if you are prepared to give up a little power to allow us to participate as partners in our own future, and in the future of the country.
>
> We want to be recognized as human beings, we don't want to spend the rest of our lives judged by negative labels that are stuck on us by other people. I am a lone parent, I'm not an irresponsible one. I'm disabled, I'm not unable. I'm unemployed, but I'm not unemployable, with a little co-operation and willingness from employers. We are increasingly called "the underclass." I believe we are undervalued and very much underestimated.[1]

Often when people think of social involvement, they think of providing something that will meet people's needs in some way. We will *do* something *for* the poor. We will provide for them food, furniture, help, education, skills, or whatever. These can all be good starting points. But we need to go further. Poverty is about marginalization and powerlessness. And some forms of charitable intervention can leave people marginalized. They can reinforce a sense of powerlessness. Something is done *for* the poor. They remain passive. They are not becoming contributors to society. They become more dependent on others. So social involvement is more than presenting people with solutions. Good social involvement is helping people to find their *own* solutions. We want people to be proactive in their lives and to regain their God-given dignity

---

[1] Tulo Raistrick, *Church, Community and Change: The Manual*, Part 2 (Teddington London: Tearfund, 2000), 10–11.

as human beings made to contribute to community life. So at the heart of good social action is the participation of those in need.

This means that time is more important than money in social involvement. That is because social involvement is about changing people, attitudes, and structures rather than simply providing goods and services. This applies to projects, but also to individual relationships. Consider this example, one based on a real situation. A church has contact with a refugee, a single parent with nine children. You can see that she needs a washing machine. You could turn up one day with one. That would be a lovely surprise. But it may not be what she needs most. You have not involved her in the decision-making process. She has not decided what kind of washing machine she wants or even whether this is the main priority. She is simply the passive recipient of your charity. She becomes dependent on you. But suppose instead that you worked with her to mend the broken relationship with her social worker and to access her rights. It would be more hassle for her and more hassle for you. You could give her a washing machine tomorrow, while this alternative route might take months. But in the long term it is enabling her to be independent. It is giving her dignity and responsibility. It is more likely to lead to lasting change.

It may be helpful to make a distinction between welfare and development. Welfare is an approach that involves giving something to the poor, like food, clothing, or skills. Development involves working with the poor to help them define their problems and find their own solutions to them. Welfare has a role, both in emergency situations and as a way of building relationships within a community. But if we never move beyond welfare, then we can create dependency. We can actually reinforce the hopelessness, powerlessness, and lack of dignity of the poor.

Consider what happens when a worker leaves or a project finishes. In the case of welfare, everything stops. No more assistance comes to the community. Or a water pump, for example, might continue to provide water, but only until it breaks down or the water table drops. Meanwhile other problems go unaddressed. But with good development the community goes on developing, and it goes on addressing new problems. This is how an Indian villager described community development: "Once individual people and the village where they live have got self-respect and control over their lives, there can be no going back. In the end, sustainability comes from what people can do for themselves."[2]

Under the Khmer Rouge all intellectuals of Cambodia were killed along with anyone who stood out from the crowd. The education system had broken down and no one dared to express personal views. Simon Batchelor had been part of a community development program after the fall of Khmer Rouge. Returning to evaluate progress he describes the following conversation with a Khmer villager:

> Mr Ee told me proudly that the people of the village no longer worried about food or the rain. "You know," he said, "when you first came two years ago we had two (open) wells for our water, and our rice depended only on the rain. Now this village has nearly one hundred machine pumps (pumping from ground water) and over one hundred foot pumps. The people do not worry about food and do not fear the rain."

Pumps had been installed; they were working well and providing people with water for irrigation. This is good welfare. But the quote continues:

> "But," he went on, "I worry about the year 2000. By that time we may have nearly 400 pumps and I wonder if there is enough water under the ground for that many pumps. What do you think and what should we do?" I sat stunned. I knew this man only two years ago, when he never volunteered a thought. Now, not only was he thinking about four years into the future (generally unheard of in rural people worldwide), but he was anticipating a possible problem and trying to proposition information to solve it before it ever started. Certainly his thinking had changed.[3]

[2] Tine Jaeger, *Community Health Development*, Tearfund Position Paper (London, 2000).
[3] From Simon Batchelor, *Transforming the Mind by Wearing Hats! Agriculture, Business and Community Development* (London: Tearfund, 1996).

This is good community development. This rural development program in Cambodia identified four factors that impeded change: the legacy of political terror, loss of personal dignity, tradition, and religious fear. Together these discouraged people from taking initiatives. The program began by trying to convince people that they themselves could make decisions. They would not receive a solution from an outside "expert." In a particular village the program facilitator would call the community together to decide upon a small project. They could decide to do whatever they wanted. The only limit was financial, with only a small amount of money made available. If this first step failed, it was still seen as a step forward because it provided a basis for future discussion. A committee was appointed from within the community, which met in public so there was always accountability. The facilitator also spent time with the villagers building up trust. Over time, using this approach the program led to the installation of over two thousand water pumps; the formation of self-supporting drilling teams and pump manufacturers; the establishment of hundreds of vegetable gardens; new crop experiments; the distribution of over one hundred buffalo; the founding of several family spacing clinics staffed by volunteers; tree planting; action on domestic violence; and the use of appropriate technology like solar driers.[4]

Strengthening the Weak

In Ezekiel 34 God condemns "the shepherds of Israel," a reference to her leaders. They have failed to care for the people and instead have exploited them for their own gain. He says: "The weak you have not strengthened, the sick you have not healed, the injured you have not bound up, the strayed you have not brought back, the lost you have not sought, and with force and harshness you have ruled them" (v. 4). So God says that he is against the shepherds of Israel and instead he himself will "strengthen the weak": "I will seek the lost, and I will bring back the strayed, and I will bind up

---

[4] Sheila Melot and Simon Batchelor, *Getting People Thinking* (London: Tearfund, 1999).

the injured and I will strengthen the weak, and the fat and the strong I will destroy. I will feed them in justice" (v. 16).

"Strengthening the weak" is a great summary of what good social involvement is about. Social involvement cannot be simply about providing goods or services to the poor. Good social involvement takes place when the poor are enabled to make choices and bring about change. Poverty creates hopelessness and powerlessness, which demean the dignity that God has given people and denies them the opportunity to work and serve others. The poor internalize their powerlessness as hopelessness; they internalize their oppression as a lack of self-confidence. Bryant Myers describes the goal of development as "changed people and just and peaceful relationships." He goes on: "By "changed people" I mean people who have discovered their true identity as children of God and who have recovered their true vocation as faithful and productive stewards of gifts from God for the well-being of all."[5]

But restoring dignity and strengthening the weak cannot be an end in itself. We are not in the business of shifting power from one place to another. Yesterday's oppressed too often become today's oppressors. This is not the goal of Christian development. Strengthening the weak as an end in itself can lead to conflict or frustration. We want people to regain dignity and make choices, but we want them to make choices for the community as a whole. God's intention for humanity was that we should rule over creation. As a result of sin, however, we have redefined rule in selfish and tyrannical ways. But God's rule is not tyrannical. God's rule brings freedom, life, peace, justice, and blessing. It was the lie of the Serpent that God's rule was tyrannical. And we have modeled human rule in the image of that lie. But Jesus redefines the rule of God for us. He comes as God's anointed King but says that he has come not to be served but to serve and to give his life as a ransom for many (Mark 10:45). He rules in love and through sacrifice. Strengthening the weak is about enabling people to exercise their

---

[5] Myers, *Walking with the Poor*, 14.

God-given rule over creation for the good of all. That is what stewardship is, not the perverted form of stewardship characteristic of some Western Christianity, which justifies whatever is good for money in the name of stewardship. But true biblical stewardship is to use the resources of creation for the good of all, including future generations.

Empowering people for service can take place among those who are not converted. Though marred by sin, people are still made in the image of God and are still the recipients of God's common grace. Many Third World cultures have a more instinctive communal orientation than that of Western individualism. But human nature is inherently selfish, and this means development is never a completed task. It is the grace of God in Jesus Christ that provides the most fundamental reorientation of a person from self or a narrow group (family, tribe) to God and to others. We are called to be beings in community just as God exists as a trinitarian community of persons. The goal of development cannot be the autonomous individual of Western liberalism. Independency is not the replacement of dependency. Nor is the goal the creation of a community that excludes the other but an inclusive community that mirrors the gracious community of the Trinity.

Daniel was born in Jalalpa, one of the many slums of Mexico City. His father abandoned the family, and his mother turned to drink and to men. To provide for himself and his siblings, Daniel got a job running orders for the tradesmen who operate outside Mexico's prisons. With a bribe to the guard, children like Daniel supply alcohol, cigarettes, and even women to the inmates. In time Daniel was caught and sent to a young offenders' institution. The judge ordered that on his release he should not live with his mother. But after a short time with his grandmother, he returned to his mother to care for his siblings. One day his half-blind brother was killed in a road accident. Enslaved by his mother and full of guilt about his brother, Daniel was left distraught and suicidal.

Armonia is a Christian agency working among the poor of Mexico. Saul Cruz, who cofounded Armonia with his wife, Pilar, teaches a course for development professionals. On one occasion the course participants questioned whether the work of Armonia could really bring genuine change to the poor of Jalalpa. So the group visited their urban transformation center and Saul invited them to talk to any of the children. They picked out a respectable-looking boy, thinking that he did not come from the slum and that they had rumbled Saul's claims. It was Daniel.

Saul and Pilar had met Daniel at the funeral of his brother. They invited him back to the center for a meal and invited him to join in the center's activities. They confronted his mother and threatened her with legal action if she did not stop demanding money from her children. Daniel graduated from the center's homework clubs and was given an Armonia scholarship. With strong, loving discipline, Daniel has prospered and looks set to go to university. In the context of a caring community, he has become a Christian and participates in the center's work with younger children.

I met Daniel at the Armonia youth club. Over pizza—a special treat—I asked the teenagers about their dreams. One told me they hoped a generation touched by the work of Armonia would bring change to the city through the Word of God. Another talked of the seed planted in them driving out the darkness of Jalalpa. A third wanted to see families change through their children. Their dreams were not those of many young people—dreams for success and prosperity. Instead, they hoped to bring change to their communities through the Word of God. These young people had been empowered by the acceptance, confidence, and education they had received from Armonia and above all by the gospel. Now they wanted to serve their community. Most of the workers within Armonia are from the community and have come through its programs.

Participation

Participation is crucial in social involvement among the poor. "A recent worldwide study of programmes that really worked and really lasted showed that participation was the single most important reason for success."[6] Participation involves people taking part in decisions and actions that affect their lives. Participation is a good thing in its own right, for it is the recognition that gives people dignity as image bearers of God. But it is also the means by which the poor are enabled to make choices and learn to be contributors to their family and community. It gives people a sense of ownership and commitment. People gain confidence and hope when their contributions are valued and when their participation leads to change.

> I was visiting development projects, and a Community Development Officer (CDO) took me to one particular village which obviously had numerous problems. On the health side, things were very bad—the people suffered from all types of worms, malaria and bilharzia, and there was no clinic. There was a school, but the building was very poor and the teachers were nearly always absent. The CDO organized a village meeting to discuss the needs of the people. "Our top priority is to make a football field," the villagers said. I was amazed and appalled. "Good," replied the CDO to the villagers. "That's a good idea." The villagers made their football field, started playing football, and organized matches against other villages. Having their own football team was a turning point in the life of the village. They had gained self-confidence, a structure for communicating with one another, and a sense that they were capable of changing things themselves. Later on they started to tackle "more important" projects to improve life in the village. But were they really more important?[7]

Participation also enables local knowledge to be included in development. The community has a past. It has stories of success and failure. It has things of which it is rightly proud. It has knowledge of its locality. If we ignore such things, our work will be less effective and will have negated an important resource of the community—its own heritage.

---

[6] Ted Lankester, *Setting Up Community Health Programmes*, 2nd ed. (London: Macmillan, 2000), 10.
[7] Source unknown.

A health worker with a college degree was working in rural Mexico. One day a father asked if he could heal his son. The boy, whose name was Pepe, was crippled by polio. The health worker suggested crutches, but the father explained that they were too far from the city to get crutches. "Then why don't we try to make some crutches?" said the health worker. The health worker searched the forest for two forked branches. As he set to work the father said: "They won't work." The health worker frowned. "Wait and see!" he said. But when Pepe put his weight on the finished crutches, they doubled and broke. "I tried to tell you they wouldn't work," said the father, "it's the wrong kind of tree." He took the machete and came back from the forest with two forked sticks of jutamo wood. When the new crutches were finished, Pepe's father tested them by putting his full weight on them. They held him easily, yet were lightweight. By afternoon, Pepe was walking with them. But they rubbed him under the arms so Pepe's father padded the crosspieces with wild kapok. As the health worker left, the whole family came to say goodbye. "I can't thank you enough," said the father. "It's I who must thank you," said the health worker. "You have taught me a great deal."[8]

Participatory Reflection and Action (PRA) has developed as a common approach to foster the participation of communities. PRA is a toolkit of *methods*—exercises and activities such as ranking, mapping, timelines, calendars, case studies, and transect walks, which have developed as ways of facilitating community participation. But it is also certain *approaches* and *behaviors*. PRA is more than running certain exercises. It is about how you approach social involvement and how you value the contribution of the poor. It is a question of whether people matter more to you than your plans and objectives.

Dr. Ted Lankester, a specialist in community health, says: "The biggest block to participation is not the unwillingness of the community. It is the possessive attitude of the health workers wanting to gain credit and keep control."[9] We cannot help the poor if we

---

[8] Edited from David Werner, *Disabled Village Children: A Guide for Community Health Workers, Rehabilitation Workers, and Families*, 2nd ed. (Berkeley, CA: Hesperian Foundation, 1999), A1–A2.
[9] Lankester, *Setting Up Community Health Programmes*, 13.

think we know best; if we want to be in control; if we want to look good. But we can help the poor if we ourselves are poor in spirit; if we mourn over our sin and the effects of sin in society; if we are meek; if we hunger for justice. We must follow the example of sacrifice and service modeled in the cross. And that means not seeking power to help, but helping to empower.

It is too easy for participation to focus on the dominant or articulate. It is usually quicker, and it is easier, but by definition such people are not the poorest. To be truly participatory we must self-consciously include the marginalized and excluded. We need to recognize that there are marginalized people within marginalized communities. Without, for example, the participation of women, otherwise well-intentioned projects have left them worse off. Agricultural projects have diverted land used for subsistence farming by women to cash production from which men have benefited. "Women's projects" do not necessarily help the situation. Income-generating projects for women have sometimes increased the burden of women's work while men have controlled the extra income. So, more important than women-specific projects is to consider the involvement of women in the development process as a whole and its impact on gender and family relationships. We need to consider women's *strategic needs*—their status and rights in a community—alongside their *practical needs*. The same principles apply to children, the elderly, and the handicapped.

ActionAid has developed a participatory approach to teaching adult literacy, building on the work of the Brazilian educationalist Paulo Freire, called REFLECT, which stands for "Regenerated Freirean Literacy through Empowering Community Techniques." Freire argued that adults learn best when they can share their experience and when their learning is clearly applicable to their lives. People's emotions need to be engaged, so you start with issues that generate energy and excitement in a community. These are presented to the community through what Freire called "codes"—posters, plays, photographs, songs, games—for the community to discuss. I visited a Christian development project in

Mexico that had performed a play about corruption ("a code"). This started a lively discussion; the community got excited because this code connected with the reality of their lives. Together they talked about what could be done. Finally the project workers acted out the story of Zacchaeus, turning the discussion on corruption into a powerful gospel presentation.

The REFLECT approach does not use textbooks. Instead each group creates its own learning materials. The group might, for example, work together to create a map of their village. These materials are copied into participants' exercise books. During the discussion several words will have been used repeatedly (house, field, river). Some of these are chosen, written on a blackboard, and broken down into syllables. The group discovers other words they can make using the syllables. Not only does this approach energize their literacy learning, but also the community begins to discuss their community so that other activities develop alongside the literacy work. By the end, each group will have produced twenty to thirty maps, calendars, charts, and diagrams, which are then used by the community to plan development activities. Three trial programs in Uganda, Bangladesh, and El Salvador proved twice as effective at teaching literacy as traditional methods. They also promoted wider development and increased participation in community organizations.[10]

There is a well-known Chinese proverb that captures well the essence of the development worker's contribution to the process of development:

> Go in search of your people:
> love them;
> learn from them;
> plan with them;
> serve them;
> begin with what they have;
> build on what they know.

---

[10] From Isabel Carter, "REFLECT: A PLA Approach to Literacy," *Footsteps* 29 (December 1996): 11–12.

But of the best leaders,
when their task is accomplished
and their work is done,
the people all remark:
"We have done it ourselves."

Summary

Good social involvement involves more than providing for the poor. We want people to regain their God-given dignity as human beings made to contribute to community life. So at the heart of good social action is the participation of those in need.

In this chapter we have considered what our attitude to the powerless should be. In the next chapter we turn to look at our attitude to the powerful.

Following the Crucified Lord

Christians are called to follow the way of the cross. The cross defines what discipleship means for us. Jesus said: "If anyone would come after me, let him deny himself and take up his cross and follow me" (Mark 8:34). Not enough attention has been given to thinking through what the way of the cross means for Christian social involvement. In chapter 9 we saw how powerlessness and marginalization are at the root of poverty. Often it is assumed that if Christians can get their hands on the levers of power, then all will be well. The following quotes suggest otherwise:

- Power tends to corrupt and absolute power corrupts absolutely. Great men are almost always bad men. (Lord Acton)
- The love of liberty is the love of others; the love of power is the love of ourselves. (William Hazlett)
- There are in the world two powers—the sword and the spirit. And the spirit has always vanquished the sword. (Napoleon)
- Nothing will so avail to divide the church as love of power. (John Chrysostom)
- We have no power from God unless we live in the persuasion that we have none of our own. (John Owen)

In 1 Corinthians 1:18–2:5 Paul explores the issues of power and weakness, with the cross as the defining model for Christians' conduct. God's power, says Paul, is revealed in weakness. God's wisdom is revealed in folly. God's glory is revealed in shame. God's victory is revealed in defeat. But Paul goes further. He applies the cross to his own ministry (1 Cor. 2:1–5). The cross is not only at the heart of our salvation. It should be at the heart of our ministries. Christian ministry is not conducted through political power or media influence. It is conducted in the upside-down, unpredictable power of the cross. It is conducted through weakness and dishonor.

In Galatians 6:12–17 Paul specifically makes the cross the model for our relationship to the world. He begins: "Those who want to make a good showing in the flesh who would force you to be circumcised, and only in order that they may not be persecuted for the cross of Christ" (v. 12). Paul had written the letter to the Galatians to counter people who were trying to compel the Galatians to be circumcised. This, Paul reveals, is not because they believed in justification by works (although, as the rest of the letter indicates, that is where Paul thinks their teaching will lead). They want to compel circumcision "to avoid being persecuted for the cross of Christ"—hence the desire to make "a good impression outwardly." They are concerned with being accepted by the wider community. "For even those who are circumcised do not themselves keep the law, but they desire to have you circumcised that they may boast in your flesh" (v. 13). These people want to be able to boast about the Galatians's "flesh," that is, the fact that they have been circumcised. They want to be able to say to the wider, persecuting Jewish community: We are okay; we are respectable.

But we are not respectable, says Paul: "But far be it from me to boast except in the cross of our Lord Jesus Christ, by which the world has been crucified to me, and I to the world. For neither circumcision counts for anything, nor uncircumcision, but a new creation. And as for all who walk by this rule, peace and mercy be upon them, and upon the Israel of God" (vv. 14–16). Our boast is the cross—the ultimate symbol of shame. Two thousand years of religious art mean we have lost the sense of the shame of the cross. Josephus describes it as "the most miserable of deaths," "the worst extreme of the tortures inflicted upon slaves," an "accursed thing," and a "plague."[1] Michael Gorman comments: "Crucifixion was first-century Rome's most insidious and intimidating instrument of power and political control. . . . It was Rome's tortuous, violent method of handling those who were perceived to threaten the empire's 'peace and security.' . . . To suffer crucifixion was to suffer the most shameful death possible."[2] Moreover, in Jewish thought the cross was associated with the curse of God. Paul has already said in Galatians that everyone hung on a tree is cursed (3:13). It would be like making the tyres used in the necklace killings of South Africa the mark of your religion. It is not only a gruesome way to die; it is also the mark of a traitor. Yet Paul says that our identity as Christians is in the cross. We boast in what is unrespectable. And once a community has shunned you in this way, it has no more social pressure it can bring to bear. You have died to the world. What the world thinks of us is meaningless to us now. All that counts is a new creation. Gorman again: "Centering on the cross was . . . an inherently anti-imperial posture that unashamedly challenged the priorities and values of the political, social, and religious status quo."[3]

Paul concludes: "From now on let no one cause me trouble, for I bear on my body the marks of Jesus" (6:17). The mark of Jesus is not circumcision but our willingness to serve, suffer, and sacrifice as he did. Paul may be referring to the mark with which slaveowners branded their slaves. It is clear from 2 Corinthians 11 that Paul could quite literally strip to the waist and relate the story of his ministry by pointing to the scars scattered across his body. Christians are to be those who have taken up their cross and followed the Crucified One. And this has big implications for our social and political involvement.

---

[1] Cited in Michael J. Gorman, *Cruciformity: Paul's Narrative Spirituality of the Cross* (Grand Rapids, MI: Eerdmans, 2001), 5.
[2] Ibid.
[3] Ibid.

From Christendom to the Cross

In AD 312, the Roman emperor Constantine saw a vision in the sky shortly before a battle. Eusebius, the church historian who wrote at the time of Constantine, described it like this: "[Constantine] said that about noon . . . he saw with his own eyes the trophy of a cross of light in the heavens, above the sun, and bearing the inscription, 'Conquer by this.' . . . In his sleep the Christ of God appeared to him with the same sign which he had seen in the heavens, and commanded him . . . to use it as a safeguard in all engagements with his enemies."[4] How real Constantine's conversion was is not clear, and there is some doubt over Eusebius's account of it. But whatever form it took, it had a profound effect on the history of the church. The following year Constantine issued the Edict of Milan, which gave religious freedom to "Christians and all others." Christians especially were to be allowed to continue as Christians without hindrance or trouble. Soon Constantine was positively encouraging Christians and giving imperial funds to the church. Sunday became the legal day of rest in the empire. It became advantageous to be a Christian. The emperor gave special favors to cities that converted *en masse*. Then the empire started to destroy pagan temples. Within a generation the church went from being a countercultural sect to the established state church. It went from being a persecuted minority to a persecuting majority. Its number rose dramatically to about 50 percent of the empire by the end of the fourth century.

Christendom was born. *Christendom* is the term used to refer to those countries and regions that consider themselves Christian. It involves the church using or influencing political power to protect its interests and further its mission. Although there were some dissident voices, for fifteen hundred years Christendom was the dominant political model in Western Europe and beyond. Even in the United States, where church and state are formally separate, the Christendom model has been a powerful

---

[4] Eusebius, *The Life of the Blessed Emperor Constantine*, 1.28–29.

influence.[5] And it was this model that was exported in the missionary expansion of the nineteenth and twentieth centuries. The relationship between colonial expansion and missionary endeavor in the nineteenth and twentieth centuries is complex. Sometimes mission was the tool of colonialism, often the beneficiary of colonialism, and sometimes the critic of colonialism. But, argues David Smith, it was not a new model: "The arrival of Columbus in the New World in 1492 was without doubt an event of enormous significance, but rather than marking the commencement of what we might call an 'imperial' model of mission, it merely represented the attempt to extend that model beyond the confines of Europe *where it had held sway for centuries.*"[6]

But today Christendom is a spent force. Secularism has pushed Christian influence out of the corridors of power. Europe can no longer be considered Christian territory—if indeed it ever was. Mission no longer takes place "over there." Europe is a mission field in which people know little of the Bible and in which the gospel has little impact on public life. David Smith says: "Christendom's division of the world and its peoples into two great blocs—*here* a culture shaped by the Gospel; *there* a realm of ignorance and darkness (a categorization that continued to inform the Western mind in various secularized reworkings)—has increasingly seemed to be implausible and unbelievable."[7] Douglas Hall says: "To say that Christianity in the world at large is undergoing a major transition is to indulge in understatement. What is happening is nothing less than the winding down of a process that was inaugurated in the fourth century of the common era."[8]

Some bemoan its passing; others are disoriented; many live in denial. Douglas Hall again:

> What is lacking in nearly all of the formerly prominent Christian
> bodies of the West is just this awareness and acceptance of their

---

[5] Douglas John Hall, *The End of Christendom and the Future of Christianity* (Harrisburg, PA: Trinity Press, 1995).
[6] David Smith, *Mission after Christendom* (London: Darton, Longan & Todd, 2003), 3.
[7] Ibid., 4.
[8] Hall, *The End of Christendom*, 1.

changed relation to power. Rather, they cling to their accustomed *modus operandi*, their imagined status vis-à-vis the powerful, and in doing so they forfeit the opportunities for truth telling and justice that historical providence is affording them. Thus, too many attempts at faith's confession simply do not "come off" because they still assume a Constantinian framework. They speak as though from positions within the power centres of society. They presuppose a certain right to assume the stand that they promulgate. Therefore they almost always fail to convince anyone outside the fold or even raise significant questions.[9]

Hall makes similar criticisms of church structures. We are so enmeshed in the privileges of Christendom that we cannot imagine an alternative to the sinking ship. "One suspects that much of our ecclesiology and church polity is informed by a process of corporate rationalization aimed at justifying the status quo."[10] What Hall says of the church at a national level can be said, too, at a congregational level. Congregational structures and relationships with the surrounding community assume a Christendom model, even in many nonstate churches. Much evangelism is dependant on rights of passage and church going as a social norm, both rapidly dwindling phenomena. We assume a certain privileged position within the local community that is no longer ours.

But in truth the demise of Christendom is an opportunity for the church to recover more truly its calling in the world. Some Christians have seen the rise of Christendom as good news, even as the church's coming of age. Eusebius, one of the first church historians, saw the conversion of Constantine as the establishment of the kingdom of God: "Invested as [Constantine] is with the appearance of heavenly sovereignty, he directs his gaze above and frames his earthly government according to the pattern of that Divine original, feeling strength in its conformity to the rule of God."[11] But Jerome gives a very different picture at the end of the

---

[9] Ibid., 2.
[10] Ibid., 7.
[11] Eusebius, *Oration* 3.5.

fourth century. He says that the church "grew through persecution and was crowned with martyrdom; and then, after reaching the Christian emperors . . . it increased in influence and wealth, but decreased in Christian virtues."[12]

With the coming of Christendom a divide grew between clergy and laity. People no longer contributed to meetings; now they had to keep quiet. The church gathered in a special building that reinforced this clergy-laity division. We get instructions like the following: "Let the lay men sit on the other side in all quietness and good order. If anyone is found sitting out of his place, let him be rebuked by the deacon. . . . Let the deacons oversee the people to stop people whispering, sleeping, laughing or nodding for everyone ought to stand wisely and attentively."[13] We start to see a reaction against this with the rise of the monastic movement and ascetics going into the desert to pursue notions of a pure Christian life. If you wanted to follow Christ, the idea was, you no longer simply joined the church; now you joined a monastery. But these were movements for the elite. John Zens identifies four tragic shifts that took place with the establishment of Christendom:[14]

1) The church portrayed in the New Testament was a dynamic organism, a living body with many parts. The church from around AD 180 onwards became an increasingly hardened institution with a fixed and complex hierarchy.

2) The early church was marked by the manifestation of a polyform ministry by which edification and the meeting of needs were accomplished through the gifts of all the brethren. The post-apostolic church moved more and more toward a uniform conception of church offices, which separated ministry from the laity and limited significant ministry to the clergy.

3) The church of the first and most of the second centuries was characterized by cycles of intense difficulty and persecution—it was a suffering body. With the advent of Constantine the

---

[12] Jerome, 'The Life of Malchus, the Captive Monk,' *Nicene and Post-Nicene Fathers*, Series II, Volume 6, ed. Philip Schaff (Peabody, MA.: Hendrickson, 1999), 315.

[13] *Apostolic Constitutions*, 2.58 (c. AD 385).

[14] John Zens, "Four Tragic Shifts in the Visible Church 180-400 AD," *Searching Together* 21 (1993): 1–4.

church became protected, favoured, and ultimately sanctioned as the state religion by the Roman state and thus became an institution at ease.

4) In the New Testament, the church, with no small measure of vulnerability, depended on the Holy Spirit to hold the brethren together and to lead them in ministry. Later, the church trusted in itself as a very powerful institution, along with its many rules, rites, and offices, to secure visible unity among its adherents.

But Christendom not only corrupted how the church saw itself. It also corrupted the church's relationship with the world. Kenneth Myers describes Christendom as "a generally friendly cultural setting for the church."[15] Prima facia this may be the case. Christendom afforded the church certain privileges and protection. But at what cost? The Dutch theologian Hendrikus Berkhof says: "To a great extent official church history is the story of the *defeats* of the Holy Spirit."[16] Those who follow the way of the cross must choose weakness instead of power, shame instead of glory. But Christendom chose power and glory. The church became aligned with the establishment so that those who were marginalized within society were therefore marginalized from the church. Christendom extends God's kingdom through the sword of political power rather than trusting in the power of the Word and the Spirit.

So the end of Christendom is an opportunity for the church. Kenneth Myers says: "The death of Christendom (or the death of a supposed "Christian America") is an opportunity to preach Christ clearly without the confusion of cultural assumptions."[17] Douglas Hall goes further: "Today Christendom is in its death throes, and the question we all have to ask ourselves is whether we can get over regarding this as a catastrophe and begin to experience it as a doorway—albeit a narrow one—into a future that is more in keep-

---

[15] Kenneth A. Myers, "A Better Way: Proclamation Instead of Protest," in *Power Religion: The Selling Out of the Evangelical Church?* ed. Michael S. Horton (Chicago: Moody, 1992), 55.
[16] Cited in Hall, *The End of Christendom*, 18.
[17] Myers, "A Better Way," 55.

ing with what our Lord first had in mind when he called disciples to accompany him on his mission to redeem the world through love, not power."[18] The church cannot return to Christendom nor should it. But fifteen hundred years is a long time. Christendom has become an instinct for many Christians, a habit that cannot be broken easily. Samuel Escobar talks of "imperial missiology," which undertakes Christian mission "from a position of superiority: political, military, financial, technological."[19] Escobar argues that a direct line can be traced between mission through the sword in the Iberian missions of the sixteenth century, mission through commerce in the nineteenth century, and mission through information technologies in the North American missions of the twentieth century.

There is no doubting the profound impact the gospel has had on Western culture. But to claim that we live in a Christian country, that its victories are God's victories, and that the state should defend Christian truth, is to confuse the rule of the state with the rule of God. God rules through his Word. The kingdom of God is not advanced or defended through the sword of political power but through the Word of God and the faithful testimony of believers. As an act of love of neighbor, it is right to want biblical values to be reflected in public life. But we should not expect the state to defend the church or its doctrines. We should not expect it to afford us special privileges. Indeed, if we read the book of Revelation seriously, we should expect the state to persecute us. If we try to create Christendom then we deny the cross.

The irony is that those who continue to cling most tenaciously to the remnants of Christendom are often from within evangelicalism when Christendom is so self-evidently an unevangelical model. Evangelicals are defined by their commitment to the centrality of the gospel. For them the sufficiency of God's Word is central. But for some reason, when we engage in the political and social realm, many of us look to the state to defend Christianity.

---

[18] Hall, *The End of Christendom*, ix.
[19] Cited in David Smith, "The Cross in Mission and Ministry," unpublished paper.

The Word is no longer sufficient to defend the name of Christ or the cause of his kingdom. We evoke the notion of a Christian society or Christian heritage when evangelicals of all people should know that people and communities are Christian only through faith in Christ. No amount of legislation can create a Christian society.

The sad reality of this is that our political engagement becomes focused on self-centeredness. Kenneth Myers says: "Surely we ought to be more preoccupied with serving our neighbours than with ruling them. The involvement of Christians in cultural and civic life ought to be motivated by love of neighbour, not by self-interest—not even by the corporate self-interest of the evangelical movement."[20]

At the time when legislation was being considered in the UK Parliament to deregulate Sunday trading laws, a friend told me he had never felt so strongly about an issue before. The legislation would have allowed shops to open on a Sunday. A campaign was mounted by the churches in the United Kingdom that led to the legislation being defeated. It was hailed at the time as an unprecedented example of what Christian social involvement could achieve. In fact, Sunday trading laws were deregulated soon after. There are good reasons for restricting Sunday trading. The defense of workers' rights was cited at the time, but the fact that evangelicals did not leap to the defense of workers on other issues suggests this was not the main motivation behind their involvement in the issue. It would be good to think that it was motivated by a desire to limit the consumption that increasingly defines our identity in the West, but the negligible difference in patterns of consumption between Christians and their non-Christian neighbors suggests that this was not a primary motive either. The reality is that much of the interest in the campaign was a legacy of Christendom fueled by a sense of self-interest. My friend told me that for the first time in his life, he was prepared to march on the streets in protest. To

---

[20] Myers, "A Better Way," 55.

which I could only reply: "Do you really feel more strongly about Sunday trading than about the twenty thousand–plus children who die each Sunday—and every other day of the week—because of poverty?"

Where does this leave social involvement? We cannot recreate Christendom, nor should we. Yet, as we have seen, Christ is Lord over every area of life. His lordship should impact education, business, politics, the arts, and so on. So how do we live out the lordship of Christ without recreating Christendom?

Toward a Political Theology of the Cross

The answer is to go back to the cross. What is the nature of Christ's reign? He is the crucified King. He is the King who "came not to be served but to serve, and to give his life as a ransom for many" (Mark 10:45). The one on the throne of history is the Lamb who was slain (Rev. 5:5–6). This is how we must live out the lordship of Christ in our social involvement: through service and sacrificial love. God told the exiles in Babylon to "seek the welfare of the city where I have sent you into exile" (Jer. 29:7), so Daniel used his political office to serve the nation of Babylon, just as Joseph had done in Egypt. The church as the church should not seek power or influence in a secular sense (2 Cor. 10:4). Instead it should seek opportunities to serve the world. As the church follows the way of the cross, it must choose "participation in the powerlessness of God in the world."[21] It stands with the weak and the powerless. It speaks out on behalf of those whose voice is not heard. It seeks justice for the poor.

This approach is in keeping with Romans 13 and 1 Peter 2. The church does not seek to usurp the God-given authority of the state by accruing to itself civil power. But this does not mean it never challenges the state to exercize its God-given authority in a godly way. The church confronts the state as it declares a different set of values through its words and deeds among the poor and as it

---

[21] Dietrich Bonhoeffer, *Letters and Papers from Prison*, ed. E. Bethge (London: SCM, 1951; English trans. 1953, 1971), 362

models those values in its community life. The subversive nature of its message is inevitable, since it proclaims to those in power the values of weakness and foolishness. It sings of a time when the proud will be scattered, rulers deposed, the humble raised, the hungry filled, and the rich sent away empty (Luke 1:51–53).

As it gives witness to the good news of the kingdom in this way, it may well be that it is persecuted. The church enters the political realm not to make itself powerful or secure but to be weak and vulnerable in love, to be in solidarity with those who are weak and powerless. The power of the kingdom is seen under the sign of the cross. This is the way the church exercises the power and lordship of God. The kingdom of God is, in the words of the Reformers, *tectum sub cruce et sub contrario*—"hidden under the cross and that which is contrary." Melba Maggay says: "The church has no need to play politics in order to wield influence. Simply by being itself, by being true to the power of its convictions and the purity of its purposes, it has power. Its authority lies in its own capacity to persuade others to believe in the integrity of its propaganda, not in the acquisition of political clout by descending to the level of a power bloc."[22]

This allows us to ask some hard questions about Christian social and political involvement:

- Do we serve ourselves or others?
- Do we seek influence for the sake of influence or to serve those in need?
- Do we accumulate the trappings of power?
- Do we compromise the Word for the sake of power?
- Are we trusting in human power or trusting in the Word and prayer?
- Are we building a Christian country or witnessing to the coming reign of God?
- Do we think the cause of the gospel will be safeguarded if we have power?

---

[22] Melba Maggay, *Transforming Society* (Oxford, UK: Regnum, 1994), 44.

The Dangers of Respectability

The church has often sought respectability in the eyes of the world. We want to be acknowledged. We want to be afforded status. We want influence. We boast of our numbers in the press and to politicians. The implication is clear: "Our voice should be taken seriously. We matter." But the desire for respectability and status weakens the power of the cross.

David Smith argues that the desire of evangelicals for social and political respectability betrayed the Great Awakening from which it arose. The evangelicalism that arose from the Great Awakening of the eighteenth century was what he calls "world-transformative Christianity."[23] This was because so many of the movement's leaders were influenced by the Reformation's emphasis on the lordship of Christ over all of life. As a result, early evangelicalism intentionally—and sometimes unintentionally—had a profound social impact. In the heart of the busy Broadmeads shopping center in Bristol is the first purpose-built Methodist chapel. Sitting in the pews, imagining what it must have been like as people gathered, one is struck by the subversive nature of the eighteenth-century revival. The working people who gathered to hear the gospel were leaving the establishment church of their masters, rulers, and employers and organizing themselves in alternative social bodies. The eighteenth-century revival was largely a movement among working people, usually despised by the privileged classes.

Smith describes how Victorian evangelicalism sought to extend the appeal of evangelicalism to the privileged classes. They "were not just concerned to ensure that the form of the message would not be offensive, its *content* should assure the rich and privileged that they might attain personal salvation in Christ without the slightest hint of a threat to their 'station' in life."[24] Evangelicalism in the nineteenth century was passionately committed to caring for the poor and reforming society, but Smith concludes:

[23] David Smith, *Transforming the World? The Social Impact of British Evangelicalism* (Carlisle, UK: Paternoster, 1998), *ix*.
[24] Ibid., 17.

It is hard to avoid the conclusion that . . . evangelicalism came per-ilously close to being a religious ideology in the Marxist sense of that term. If this conclusion is correct it has serious implications in relation to secularization: . . . evangelicalism may have achieved the success it sought in renewing the Establishment, but a high price was paid for this if, by identifying the gospel with an elite culture and a deeply conservative approach to domestic politics, it alienated the growing numbers of people who were now chal-lenging the patriarchal structures of British society and calling for radical social reforms. Without intending it, the movement associated with the Clapham Sect may have been a significant fac-tor in the long-term decline of religion in the United Kingdom.[25]

The second-generation leaders of Methodism followed a simi-lar route. Despite Wesley's political conservatism, Methodism began to make an impact on the social order. Gospel freedom led to calls of political freedom. In England Wesley founded religious societies, while the leaders of the revival in Wales formed *seiats*— communities of believers who met to exhort each other and care for one another's needs. This experience gave working people skills in organization and self-help for the first time. As a result, the roots of the trade union movement and the UK Labour party lie as much in Methodism as they do in socialism. But after Wesley's death, the revival and moves for social change were, Smith dem-onstrates, suppressed by the movement's leaders in order to gain respectability. They boasted that Methodism made the poor con-tent with their lot. Often on the high streets of Britain you see Vic-torian chapels with large, colonnaded fronts. But when you look behind the finery of the front, the building itself is relatively small. These edifices of nonconformist architecture were not signs of gospel growth but a vain-glorious attempt to say: we have arrived, we are mainstream, we are respectable. There were other voices, and evangelicalism had a profound impact on political dissent. But these voices did not prevail or were subsumed in frustration into the secular labor movement.

---

[25] Ibid., 19.

Let me illustrate with the story of my friend Dave. Dave had spent two years as what is known as a "lay assistant" and was considering what to do next. He wanted to go into full-time ministry. He has a good grasp of the gospel and is an able communicator. He comes from a working-class background and had worked as a laborer before becoming a lay assistant. He was trying to decide whether to go straight into church planting or complete a theological degree. As he took advice from various people, one prominent evangelical leader told him that he needed a degree so that in future ministry he could relate to doctors, lawyers, and other professionals. Whatever the merits of academic qualifications in preparing for ministry, consider the underlying assumptions behind this advice. While a degree might enable Dave to relate to professionals, it will undoubtedly make him less able to relate to working class people and the marginalized. But the assumption is that "successful" churches are churches with professionals.

A church in a prosperous town with a population of just 27,000 received over sixty applications for a ministerial vacancy. Friends of mine ministering in poor areas despair of generating any interest in ministerial vacancies. It would be difficult to overstate how far we have come from the model of Christian communities and Christian ministry outlined by Paul in 1 Corinthians 1–2. The desire for prestige, respectability, influence, and status is strong within evangelicalism, but these are unevangelical attitudes. We need to learn again what it is go "outside the camp" (Heb. 13:13). C. B. Samuel, a development practitioner from India, says: "In 1 Corinthians 4 Paul says the Apostles are 'at the end of the procession.' They are 'the scum of the earth.' This is authentic Christian leadership. If you choose to be irrelevant you are not out of touch. You are where most of the world is. The poor of the world are not relevant. When we become the scum of the world we become what the poor already are."[26]

---

[26] C. B. Samuel and Tim Chester, "Integral Mission, Humility and Lifestyle," in *Justice, Mercy and Humility: Integral Mission and the Poor*, ed. Tim Chester (Carlisle, UK: Paternoster, 2002), 203–4.

Summary

For centuries the model of Christendom married church interests with political power. But secularization means the days of Christendom are over. This is an opportunity for the church to regain an approach to power that is shaped by the cross. Political influence and social respectability should not be important to us, because we have died to the world.

11

Can We Make a Difference?

Can we make a difference? I have a copy of a cartoon in which someone says, "What difference can one person make?" In the next frame two or three more speech bubbles have appeared asking the same question. In the final frame there are a plethora of similar speech bubbles that have sprung up across the world. The implication is clear: together we *can* make a difference. And I agree. But I want to be cautious.

I believe that by the grace of God (and only by the grace of God) I can make a difference in the lives of people I know. I believe my church can make a difference in the life of the community in which it is situated. I believe that the concerted effort of Christians can impact political and business decisions. I was part of the Jubilee 2000 campaign in its earliest days. At that point, and I hope they will forgive me for saying this, it consisted of a bunch of eccentrics dreaming impossible dreams. Four years later I shed a few tears when I was part of fifty thousand people on a sunny day in London sending a petition with twenty million signatures to world leaders who eventually agreed to cancel $100 billion of Third World debt.[1] But still I am more cautious about what all this might add up to. For many the rhetoric is that of eradicating

---

[1] See Marlene Barrett, ed., *The World Will Never Be the Same Again* (London: Jubilee 2000 Coalition, 2000); and Ann Pettifor, "Case Study: Campaigning for Macro-Policy Change: Jubilee 2000," in

poverty. More than one organization has that as a stated goal. But we will not eradicate poverty from history. History is in a state of constant flux. Sometimes we see increased social justice and moral advance, often through the actions of God's people. But in other places we see moral decline and growing inequality. The international community has agreed to a series of "millennium development goals," the headline target of which is to halve the number of people in extreme poverty by 2015. And if they galvanize action for the poor, then they will have proved their worth. Whether they are realistic, time will tell, but I confess to be skeptical.

But is it contradictory to argue for social involvement while being skeptical about eradicating poverty? It often seems axiomatic among advocates of social involvement that we should talk up what can be achieved, holding out to people the hope of ending world poverty. Duncan Forrester speaks of the need for "reigniting utopian hopes as the engine of social transformation."[2] The hope of significant change, it seems, is needed to galvanize action. How should our expectations of social change—or lack of social change—affect our commitment as Christians to getting involved?

For many it is simply a question of getting our approach right. Each new fad in the development world is lauded as the approach that will enable us to make major strides forward. David Korten, in his influential book *Getting to the 21st Century*,[3] identifies the shifting approaches of voluntary organizations. The first generation, he claims, focused on relief and welfare, directly delivering services through humanitarian assistance. While such assistance continues to have a place in emergency situations and often receives significant public support, development agencies began to recognize that it offered only temporary alleviation. The second generation focused on small-scale, self-reliant local development. They began to work in partnership with communities to facilitate

---

Justice, Mercy and Humility: Integral Mission and the Poor, ed. Tim Chester (Carlisle, UK: Paternoster, 2002), 217–27.

[2] Duncan B. Forrester, *On Human Worth: A Christian Vindication of Equality* (London: SCM, 2001), 5.

[3] David C. Korten, *Getting to the 21st Century: Voluntary Action and the Global Agenda* (Sterling, VA: Kumarian Press, 1990).

self-help projects. The focus was small and grassroots in contrast to the large-scale state projects that often produced expensive white elephants bringing little benefit to the poorest communities. Some development agencies were founded to pursue these second-generation strategies, but many others moved into them out of a disquiet with their involvement in welfare approaches. The third-generation approach grew out of the frustration of impacting only a few communities. Agencies began to get involved in advocacy, trying to influence unjust and inequitable policies and practices. Korten highlights the way these approaches coexist—often in significant tension—within development agencies. Korten himself advocates a fourth approach that shifts the focus away from Western development agencies toward indigenous civil society: organizations owned and run by local people. He sees hope in what he calls a "people's movement" for social change.

Development is a discipline with a strong sense of moral purpose, and each new approach is promoted as *the* way forward that will eradicate poverty. The assumption is that with this new stage in our thinking, we have arrived; we have discovered the secret to eradicating poverty. Advocacy, for example, is promoted on the basis that by tackling the underlying causes of poverty—the structures and practices that perpetuate injustice—we will make a deep and lasting impact. We will achieve at last what we have failed to achieve through other approaches. But Korten warns that each policy advance achieved through advocacy must be "replicated hundreds of thousands, even millions, of times, to achieve the needed transformation of the institutions of global society," and then "each individual step forward transforming a policy or institution is subject to reversal by the still larger forces generated by backward looking national and international institutions."[4] Confidence in the ability of advocacy to change the world is an unrealistic, romantic hope. The same, however, could be said of Korten's confidence in people movements. Dewi Hughes reminds

---

[4] Ibid., 123.

us that "despite all the theorizing and the actions that have flowed from it, we have to face up to the fact that the problem of poverty is as great as ever. . . . Development may have succeeded here and there, and any success must not be despised, but in global terms all the talking and working in the last 50 years has not solved the problem."[5]

The Bible has a much more realistic view of sin. The Bible recognizes that sin is a universal trait of humanity, both rich and poor. It should not surprise Christians when the exploited become the exploiters. The exploited may have a morally superior case in a particular situation, but that does not mean they are morally superior beings. And sin is not only universal; it is also deep. It penetrates our cultures and societies, affecting our social, economic, and political systems. This is what the Bible calls "worldliness." The term "world" is used in the Bible for creation as an object of God's love (John 3:16), but it is also used of human society and culture in opposition to God's will (1 John 2:15–17). Satan tempts individuals into sin and error, but the lies of Satan also affect whole cultures and, as a result, social structures. Idolatry is as much a social phenomenon as an individual act. It is communal idolatries that perpetuate poverty. As Thomas Cullinan says, "If we idolize wealth then we create poverty; if we idolize success then we create the inadequate; if we idolize power we create powerlessness."[6]

Martin Luther, the great Protestant Reformer, distinguished between "theologies of glory," which seek the revelation of God in visible displays of divine power and glory, and a "theology of the cross," which sees the ultimate revelation of God in the cross. By faith the Christian sees in the cross power in weakness, victory in failure, and glory in shame. In the same way we need to distinguish between "eschatologies of glory" and an "eschatology of the cross." Eschatologies of glory expect in the present the glory that belongs to the future. They expect to move beyond the sacrifice, suffering, and submission of the cross to perfection, glory, and

---

[5] Hughes, *God of the Poor*, 14.
[6] Source unknown.

triumph. They want power, status, and honor in the present. An eschatology of the cross, in contrast, recognizes that the kingdom of God is hidden now and that its glory lies in the future. The eschatology of the cross recognizes there is in the experience of the believer a pattern of suffering followed by glory that corresponds to the pattern of the cross and resurrection. It recognizes that life in the present is marked by the cross. The cross was not only the supreme expression of divine love; it was also the supreme expression of human evil. At the cross we discover the true depth of human sin. The resurrection of the Crucified One is the promise and the beginning of the defeat of sin and the renewal of the earth. But history still bears the mark of the cross. The world is not yet redeemed. The glory and power of the coming kingdom are present in history but in a hidden form as the shame and weakness of the gospel community. The redemption of the world as a whole is a future reality, so no part of the political spectrum can offer utopia prior to the return of Christ. As such the cross judges any claim to the establishment of that which will rightly happen only after the return of Christ.

Melba Maggay was in the forefront of evangelical involvement in the "people power" revolution that brought down the unjust Marcos regime in the Philippines. This people's revolution is often held up as a testament of what can be achieved through social action, but Maggay writes movingly of its disappointments. "'People power,'" she says, "deteriorated into distorted exercises of misguided political will by a loyal fringe screaming in the streets or a dangerously armed cadre of vigilantes let loose in the name of faith and freedom to track down communists. In politics, as in much of life, there is this tragic tendency to move towards a dark underside. . . . Scripture has an ancient name for this: sin."[7] So Maggay talks about *the practice of radical pessimism:* "Despair is the property of those who expect much, and have not yet learned the modulating pragmatism of a radical pessimism that rejoices at

---

[7] Melba Maggay, *Transforming Society* (Oxford, UK: Regnum, 1994), 96.

simply having endured while haunted by a constant sense of the possibility of failure."[8]

The failure to see the cross as the mark of human history and Christian discipleship is the main weakness of liberation theology. Liberation theology came to prominence in the 1970s. It was initially a Latin American phenomenon but has spread elsewhere. The person who first brought it to wider attention was Gustavo Gutiérrez. Gutiérrez argued that poverty does not arise from a lack of development or education but rather is the result of structural injustice. The problem is not that poorer countries are underdeveloped. The problem is their unjust dependency on the powerful countries of the West. Poverty is addressed not through occasional and paternalistic charity but through radical social change. A key theme for liberation theology is the exodus from Egypt, which is seen as a paradigm for political liberation. There is much in liberation theology that is suggestive and positive. But the fundamental problem with it is its eschatology—it expects too much now and too little for the future. Its eschatology is overrealized. It looks for the coming of the kingdom through revolution or conscientization. It must contend with the Bible's witness to a future beyond history: the return of Christ and the new creation. The kingdom of God is present in grace through the proclamation of the gospel and in the lives of cross-centered disciples. But the coming of the kingdom in power belongs to the future.

The critique offered by an eschatology of the cross can also be applied at the other end of the political spectrum to prosperity teaching. Prosperity teaching says that Christians can and should expect to be healthy and wealthy in this life. It is a common and growing phenomenon across the world with an obvious attraction in communities in which daily life is a struggle. God wills this for his people, people are promised, if only we will exercise the faith to claim it. But again such thinking fails to recognize the centrality of the cross in Christian discipleship and a Christian view of life

---

[8] Ibid., 99.

in history. Perhaps the most neglected promise of Jesus is: "In this world you will have tribulation" (John 16:33).

In the New Testament, hope is often accompanied by patience and longsuffering, themes that feature weakly in liberation theology and prosperity teaching. In his letter James writes to churches facing economic hardship. The recipients are facing "trials of various kinds" (James 1:2, 12). Though these trials seem to have taken different forms, at root they were economic. Acts 11:27–30 describes a famine that hit Palestine and which prompted the first gift from Gentile to Jewish believers. Many in the congregations would have been subsistence farmers or agricultural laborers facing hardship and exploitation as the value of their labor fell. Evidence for this is found within the letter itself. James says the rich in society are exploiting the poor within the congregation (2:6). He talks about "the brother in humble circumstances" (1:9 NIV), that is, someone who is poor and marginalized in society. His warning against favoritism makes sense, given how easy it would have been to treat a rich visitor with special honor as a potential benefactor (2:1–5). When James links faith and deeds, the example he gives matches the situation in the congregation: a wealthy Christian who mouths empty words of comfort to a needy brother or sister without doing anything to help (2:15–17). In James 5:1–6, James addresses the rich oppressors outside the church. But he wants to be overheard by those within the church. He wants those who emulate the rich to listen in; they are his real audience. "You aspire to their wealth," he says in effect, "but do you not realize their wealth has a price tag on it? The cost is ruined lives—maybe even the lives of your brothers and sisters in the church. And the cry of the oppressed has reached the ears of God." "Don't you realize," he is saying, "what God has in store for the rich who oppress: their wealth will rot and corrode, and they will be condemned. How can you aspire to be like these people?"

The community is not to aspire to be like the rich landowners who face God's judgment (5:1–6). Instead they are to "be patient . . . until the coming of the Lord" (5:7). The message to this community facing economic oppression is to be patient, to wait for the Lord's coming. Hope in the New Testament is certain hope that looks beyond history to the coming of a new creation. We should not be afraid of the accusation that this is an "other worldly" eschatology. Biblical hope does not look to another world but to the future renewal of this world. Nevertheless, it is a *future* renewal. Nor should we be afraid of declaring to the poor and oppressed the coming of a kingdom of justice and plenty. If this is "pie in the sky," then so be it; we must not minimize the extent to which "pie in the sky" is good news. It is worse to offer people hope for the imminent future that cannot be sustained in the reality of a world marred by sin.[9] Hope in the New Testament is directed beyond history to the return of Christ and the new creation. It is ultimate, not proximate. We must contend with the fact that most of the poor will remain in poverty throughout their lives. The hope of the gospel is the only hope we can offer them that will survive the vagaries of history.

Paul writes to the Thessalonians: "We continually remember before our God and Father your work produced by faith, your labor prompted by love, and your endurance inspired by hope in our Lord Jesus Christ" (1 Thess. 1:3 NIV). The work and labor of the Thessalonians are the result not of hope but of faith and love. But this does not mean hope is unimportant. Paul thanks God for the endurance of the Thessalonians, which is inspired by hope in Christ (see also Col. 1:5). That which is produced by faith and prompted by love is sustained by hope. This hope is not hope for change in this life. It is not hope that our work and labor will bring about transformations in history. Paul goes on to define Christians as those who have "turned to God from idols to serve the living and true God, and to wait for his Son from heaven, whom he raised from the dead, Jesus who delivers us from the wrath to come" (1 Thess. 1:9–10).

In Mark 14:7 (NIV) Jesus says: "The poor you will always have with you" (see also Matt. 26:11 and John 12:8). Jesus is eating at the

---

[9] See Stephen Williams, "On Giving Hope in a Suffering World: Response to Moltmann," in *Issues in Faith and History*, ed. Nigel Cameron (Edinburgh: Rutherford House, 1989), 3–19.

home of Simon the Leper when a woman pours an expensive flask of perfume over his head. Some of those attending are indignant at what they see as a waste of money. They rebuke her, saying, "This ointment could have been sold for more than three hundred denarii and given to the poor" (Mark 14:5). But Jesus defends her:

> Leave her alone. Why do you trouble her? She has done a beautiful thing to me. For you always have the poor with you, and whenever you want, you can do good for them. But you will not always have me. She has done what she could; she has anointed my body beforehand for burial. And truly, I say to you, wherever the gospel is proclaimed in the whole world, what she has done will be told in memory of her. (Mark 14:6–9)

Jesus is not saying there are more important things to spend our money on than the poor. Nor is he suggesting that the continuing presence of the poor makes care for them pointless. He commends care for the poor as a normal priority, something we can do at any time we want. Indeed John Owen, the great Puritan theologian, made this verse the foundation for the role of deacons, whom he saw as those responsible for social involvement.[10] Instead Jesus's point is to highlight the extraordinary nature of the moment. He is among them but is about to leave. He wants to direct their attention to his imminent death. Her act is a preparation for his burial, since the normal process of anointing the dead will be interrupted in the case of Jesus by his resurrection (Mark 16:1–3).

Jesus quotes from Deuteronomy 15. Moses is reiterating the law to the people of Israel as they stand on the verge of the Promised Land. He warns them not to be hard-hearted or tightfisted toward the poor, but to be openhanded (Deut. 15:7–8). He reminds them to cancel debts and release slaves every seven years. Having experienced liberation from slavery in the exodus, they are to be a liberated and liberating society (v. 15). In this context he promises: "There should be no poor among you, for in the land the Lord

---

[10]John Owen, *True Nature of a Gospel Church*, vol. 16, *The Works of John Owen* (Edinburgh: Banner of Truth, 1968), 143, 146.

your God is giving you to possess as your inheritance, he will richly bless you, if only you fully obey the LORD your God and are careful to follow all these commands I am giving you today" (vv. 4–5 NIV). When God's people live under God's rule, there will be no poor among them. God's rule is a liberating rule, a rule of justice and blessing. It is a rule of peace and prosperity. Pharaoh's rule was harsh and cruel, but the Ten Commandments are, as Chris Wright puts it, like "a bill of rights" ensuring a society of justice and equity.[11] The jubilee legislation of Deuteronomy 15 is a central dimension of that social vision.

But the book of Deuteronomy is also painfully realistic. It reflects on the faithlessness of the generation of Israelites in the wilderness, seeing it not as an aberration but as typical (Deut. 1:26–46; 6:16; 8:1–20). Moses goes on to predict the rebellion of future generations (Deut. 31:14–29). This threat of rebellion is a brooding presence in the book, underlying its repeated call to remember both what God has done in salvation and what the people had done in rebellion. So while Deuteronomy 15 promises that there will be no poor among God's people if they live under God's rule, it is also realistic enough to say: "There will never cease to be poor in the land" (Deut. 15:11). In other words, only a transformation of the rebellious heart of humanity will bring an end to poverty. Only with the reestablishment of God's rule over the earth at the return of Christ will there be justice and equity. In the meantime there will always be poor people on the earth. But far from being a reason for inaction, the *continuing* presence of the poor is the basis for the *continuing* command to be openhanded. Deuteronomy 15:11 continues: "There will never cease to be poor in the land. Therefore I command you, 'You shall open wide your hand to your brother, to the needy and to the poor, in your land.'"

Only in the eschatological future will poverty be eradicated. But even now within history this future can be glimpsed. And it is glimpsed among those people whose rebellious hearts are being

[11] Christopher J. H. Wright, *Living as the People of God: The Relevance of Old Testament Ethics* (Nottingham, UK: Inter-Varsity, 1983), 143.

transformed by the grace of the gospel. It is glimpsed in the community in which the rule of God has begun to take shape. Luke alludes to Deuteronomy 15 in his description of the first Christian community:

> Now the full number of those who believed were of one heart and soul, and no one said that any of the things that belonged to him was his own, but they had everything in common. And with great power the apostles were giving their testimony to the resurrection of the Lord Jesus, and great grace was upon them all. There was not a needy person among them, for as many as were owners of lands or houses sold them and brought the proceeds of what was sold. (Acts 4:32–34)

We cannot eradicate poverty within history. Many of our achievements are reversed and undone. But still we are commanded to care for the poor. We help the poor not because we will move humanity one step closer to a poverty-free utopia. We help the poor because they are people whom we should love. And meanwhile the jubilee community of Jesus witnesses to the coming reign of God. Our social and economic relationships are the place on earth where God's future can be seen. We are the light of the world, a city on a hill (Matt. 5:14). Melba Maggay says:

> So this we believe: a kingdom of justice and righteousness has begun, and it is making its way into people's lives and denting structures that continue to oppress and dehumanize. Such work is seldom done in the corridors of power nor in the halls of the great. Often it is in the many small acts of integrity and goodness that many faceless men and women do every day, believing that behind the face of an evil that is strong is an unseen good that is stronger, even when it wears the face of weakness. It is this daily practice of hope which keeps most of us going, keeping the monsters at bay as humbly and powerfully we are caught up in the kingdom fire and the stubborn grace that shines at the heart of existence.[12]

---

[12] Maggay, *Transforming Society*, 100.

Summary

We cannot eradicate poverty within history. Our achievements may be reversed and undone. But we still have an obligation to care for the poor as we reflect the character of God, live under the reign of God, and respond to the grace of God. Proclamation will be central to Christian involvement with the poor because the greatest need of the poor—along with all people—is to be reconciled with God through the gospel. But the message we proclaim is best understood in the context of loving actions and loving community.

We might see reform in society; we might not. The important thing is for the church to witness to the coming liberation of God. We are called to be the jubilee community in which the poor are welcomed, included, and strengthened. We are the place on earth where God's future can be seen.

"Jesus, Jewel of the Poor"

Stewart Henderson

From the crystal courts of heaven
to the fly-blown stable floor,
this a different kind of glory—
Jesus, jewel of the poor.

Visionary of unknown planets
strolls unnoticed by the shore,
this a sparse and modest glory—
Jesus, jewel of the poor.

Made the dust walk by his breathing,
weeping image of the Law.
this a strangely chosen glory—
Jesus, jewel of the poor.

Zeal of heaven hangs exhausted,
bore the gouge of Satan's claw,
this a beaten, hopeless glory—
Jesus, jewel of the poor.

Homeless Saviour of the nomad
lifts the starving through his door,
this the just and finished glory—
Jesus, jewel of the poor.[1]

---

[1] Stewart Henderson. Used with permission of the author.

Further Reading

Introduction

On the history of evangelical social involvement see David Bebbington's fine history of evangelicalism, *Evangelicalism in Modern Britain* (London: Unwin Hyman, 1989); and John Wolffe, ed., *Evangelical Faith and Public Zeal: Evangelicals and Society in Britain 1780–1980* (London: SPCK, 1995). For the more recent rediscovery of social involvement by evangelicals see Tim Chester, *Awakening to a World of Need: The Recovery of Evangelical Social Concern* (Nottingham, UK: Inter-Varsity, 1993).

Chapter 1: The Case for Social Involvement

The following are good introductory presentations of the case for Christian social involvement:

Haugen, Gary. *Good News about Injustice*. Nottingham, UK: Inter-Varsity, 1999.

Hughes, Dewi A. In collaboration with Matthew Bennett. *God of the Poor*. Carlisle, UK: OM, 1998.

Keller, Timothy J. *Generous Justice: How God's Grace Makes Us Just*. New York: Dutton, 2010.

———. *Ministries of Mercy: The Call of the Jericho Road*. Phillipsburg, NJ: P&R, 1997.

Kirk, Andrew. *A New World Coming*. London: Marshalls, 1983.

Sider, Ronald J. *Rich Christians in an Age of Hunger*. London: Hodder & Stoughton, 1977.

Stott, John. *Issues Facing Christians Today*. London: Marshall, Morgan & Scott, 1984.

Excellent, but very much at an academic level, is Oliver O'Donovan's magisterial work *Resurrection and Moral Order: An Outline for Evangelical Ethics* (Nottingham, UK: Inter-Varsity, 1986). At the other end of the scale Viv Grigg tells his own story of working in a Filipino slum and its impact on his thinking, in *Companion to the Poor* (Sydney: Albatross, 1984). For a charismatic perspective see Brian Hathaway, *Beyond Renewal: The Kingdom of God* (Milton Keynes, UK: Word, 1999). For an introduction to rights-based development see Simon Maxwell, *What Can We Do with a Rights-Based Approach to Development?* ODI Briefing Paper (London, 1999).

Chapter 2: More Than a Private Faith

Lesslie Newbigin did much to highlight the dangers of privatized faith, especially in his books: *Foolishness to the Greeks: The Gospel and Western Culture* (Grand Rapids, MI: Eerdmans, 1986); and *The Gospel in a Pluralistic Society* (London: SPCK, 1989). At a popular level see Neil Hudson, *Imagine Church: Releasing Whole-Life Disciples* (Nottingham, UK: Inter-Varsity, 2012).

On a biblical worldview based on creation, fall, redemption and consummation see:

Marshall, Paul. *Thine Is the Kingdom.* London: Marshall, Morgan & Scott, 1984. See esp. 20–38.
McCloughry, Roy. *The Eye of the Needle.* Nottingham, UK: Inter-Varsity, 1990. See esp. 99–113.
Wolters, Albert. *Creation Regained.* Carlisle, UK: Paternoster, 1985.

On using the Old Testament see Christopher J. H. Wright, *Living as the People of God: The Relevance of Old Testament Ethics* (Nottingham, UK: Inter-Varsity, 1983). Also helpful are James W. Sire, *Discipleship of the Mind* (Nottingham, Nottingham, UK: Inter-Varsity, 1990); and Robert Banks, *All the Business of Life: Bringing Theology down to Earth* (Sydney: Albatross, 1987). Richard Bauckham's *The Bible in Politics*

(London: SPCK, 1989) is a stimulating example of the application of the Bible to political issues.

Chapter 3: The Case for Evangelizing the Poor

Sadly, few books on evangelism have much to say about the poor, and few books on the poor have much to say about evangelism. Exceptions are Ron Sider, *Evangelism and Social Action* (London: Hodder & Stoughton, 1993); and John Stott, *Christian Mission in the Modern World* (Eastbourne, UK: Kingsway, 1975, 1986). For a discussion of the issues in a United Kingdom context see Tim Chester, *Unreached? Growing Churches in Working-Class and Deprived Areas* (Nottingham, UK: InterVarsity, 2012). A great introduction to evangelism is John Chapman, *Know and Tell the Gospel*, 2nd ed. (Sydney: Matthias Media, 1998).

Chapter 4: Social Involvement and Proclamation

Ronald J. Sider's *Evangelism and Social Action* and John Stott's *Christian Mission in the Modern World*, mentioned above, are good starting points, along with *Evangelism and Social Responsibility: An Evangelical Commitment*, Lausanne Occasional Paper 21, 1982, http://www.lausanne.org/en/documents/lops/79-lop-21.html; and the papers of the Grand Rapids consultation, which were published as *In Word and Deed*, ed. Bruce Nicholls (Carlisle, UK: Paternoster, 1985). For a relational approach to evangelism see Jim Peterson, *Living Proof: Sharing the Gospel Naturally* (Colorado Springs, CO: NavPress, 1989). Also worth looking at is David Bosch's magisterial book on mission, *Transforming Mission: Paradigm Shifts in Theology of Mission* (Maryknoll, NY: Orbis, 1997).

Chapter 5: Social Involvement and the Kingdom of God

Ronald J. Sider and John Stott, *Evangelism, Salvation and Social Justice* (Nottingham, UK: Grove Books, 1977) is a good introduction to the debates, although Sider has subsequently changed his position (see his *Evangelism and Social Action*, pp. 199–213). For differing perspectives see:

DeYoung, Kevin, and Greg Gilbert. *What Is the Mission of the Church? Making Sense of Social Justice, Shalom, and the Great Commission.* Wheaton, IL: Crossway, 2011.

Evangelical Quarterly 62:1 (1990), which was devoted to these issues.

Padilla, C. René. *Mission between the Times.* Grand Rapids, MI: Eerdmans, 1985.

Samuel, Vinay, and Chris Sugden, eds. *The Church in Response to Human Need.* Oxford, UK: Regnum, 1987.

Tinker, Melvin. *Evangelical Concerns.* Fearn, Ross-shire, UK: Mentor, 2001. See pp. 139–66.

See also Tim Chester, "Eschatology and the Transformation of the World: Contradiction, Continuity, Conflation and the Endurance of Hope," in *Transforming the World?*, ed. Jamie Grant and Dewi A. Hughes (Nottingham, UK: Apollos, 2009), 223–43; and, at an academic level, Tim Chester, *Mission and the Coming of God: Eschatology, the Trinity and Mission in the Theology of Jürgen Moltmann and Contemporary Evangelicalism, Paternoster Theological Monographs* (Carlisle, UK: Paternoster, 2006).

Chapter 6: Good News to the Poor

Some of the New Testament background to this chapter can be found in N. T. Wright's *The New Testament and the People of God* (London: SPCK, 1992); and in *Jesus and the Victory of God* (London: SPCK, 1996); or, in a more popular form, his book *The Original Jesus: The Life and Vision of a Revolutionary* (Grand Rapids, MI: Eerdmans, 1997).

Chapter 7: Good News to the Rich

On consumerism see Craig Bartholomew and Thorsten Moritz, eds., *Christ and Consumerism: A Critical Analysis of the Spirit of the Age* (Carlisle, UK: Paternoster, 2000); and, at a more popular level, see:

Alcorn, Randy. *The Treasure Principle: Unlocking the Secret of Joyful Giving.* Rev. ed. Colorado Springs, CO: Multnomah, 2005.

Hatmaker, Brandon. *Barefoot Church: Serving the Least in a Consumer Culture.* Grand Rapids, MI: Zondervan, 2011.

Platt, David. *Radical: Taking Back Your Faith from the American Dream*. Colorado
    Springs, CO: Multnomah, 2010.
Starkey, Mike. *Born to Shop*. Oxford, UK: Monarch, 1989.

Craig Blomberg presents a comprehensive look at the biblical material in *Neither Poverty Nor Riches: A Biblical Theology of Possessions* (Nottingham, UK: Apollos, 1999). On simple lifestyle see Ronald J. Sider, ed., *Lifestyle in the Eighties* (Carlisle, UK: Paternoster, 1982); and John V. Taylor, *Enough Is Enough* (London: SCM, 1975). On "whole life" discipleship see Tom Sine, *Mustard Seed vs. McWorld: Reinventing Life and Faith for the Future* (Oxford, UK: Monarch, 1999).

Chapter 8: Welcoming the Excluded

On understanding poverty see Simon Maxwell, *The Meaning and Measurement of Poverty, ODI Poverty Briefing* (London, 1999); Robert Chambers, *Rural Development: Putting the Last First* (London: Intermediate Technology, 1983); and, from a Christian perspective, Bryant L. Myers, *Walking with the Poor: Principles and Practices of Transformational Development* (Maryknoll, NY: Orbis, 1999). Some of the material on the role of the church is based on Steve Timmis and Tim Chester, *The Gospel-Centred Church* (London: Good Book Company, 2002).

Chapter 9: Strengthening the Powerless

Bryant Myers, *Walking with the Poor: Principles and Practices of Transformational Development* (Maryknoll, NY: Orbis, 1999) is a good place to start exploring the themes in this chapter. On different approaches to development see David C. Korten, *Getting to the 21st Century: Voluntary Action and the Global Agenda* (Sterling, VA: Kumarian Press, 1990). See also Robert D. Lupton, *Toxic Charity: How Churches and Charities Hurt Those They Help (And How to Reverse It)* (New York: HarperOne, 2011); and Brian Fikkert and Steve Corbett, *When Helping Hurts: Alleviating Poverty without Hurting the Poor . . . and Yourself* (Chicago: Moody, 2009).

On participation and participatory approaches see:

Chambers, Robert. *Whose Reality Counts? Putting the First Last*. London: Intermediate Technology, 1997.

Hope, Anne, and Sally Timmel. *Training for Transformation: A Handbook for Community Workers, Books I, II, and III*. London: Intermediate Technology, 1984.

Pretty, Jules N., Irene Guijt, John Thompson, and Ian Scoones. *Participatory Learning and Action: A Trainer's Guide*. London: International Institute for Environment and Development, 1995.

Chapter 10: Following the Crucified Lord

On advocacy see Graham Gordon, *What If I Got Involved? Taking A Stand against Social Injustice* (Carlisle, UK: Paternoster, 2003). On the end of Christendom see David Smith's *Mission after Christendom* (London: Darton, Longman & Todd, 2003). On Christian approaches to political involvement see Melba Maggay, *Transforming Society* (Oxford, UK: Regnum, 1994); John Howard Yoder, *The Politics of Jesus* (Grand Rapids, MI: Eerdmans, 1972); and Dewi A. Hughes, *Power and Poverty: Divine and Human Rule in a World of Need* (Nottingham, UK: Inter-Varsity, 2008). Not for the fainthearted is Oliver O'Donovan, *The Desire of Nations: Rediscovering the Roots of Political Theology* (Cambridge, UK: Cambridge University Press, 1996). See also David Smith, *Transforming the World? The Social Impact of British Evangelicalism* (Carlisle, UK: Paternoster, 1998).

Chapter 11: Can We Make a Difference?

Once again see Melba Maggay's fine little book *Transforming Society* (Oxford, UK: Regnum, 1994).

Selected Bibliography

Alcorn, Randy. *The Treasure Principle: Unlocking the Secret of Joyful Giving. Rev. ed.* Colorado Springs, CO: Multnomah, 2005.

Banks, Robert. *All the Business of Life: Bringing Theology Down-to-Earth.* Sydney: Albatross, 1987.

Bartholomew, Craig, and Thorsten Moritz, eds. *Christ and Consumerism: A Critical Analysis of the Spirit of the Age.* Carlisle, UK: Paternoster, 2000.

Bauckham, Richard. *The Bible in Politics.* London: SPCK, 1989.

Bebbington, D. W. *Evangelicalism in Modern Britain.* London: Unwin Hyman, 1989.

Blomberg, Craig, L. *Neither Poverty Nor Riches: A Biblical Theology of Possessions.* Nottingham, UK: Apollos, 1999.

Bosch, David. *Transforming Mission: Paradigm Shifts in Theology of Mission.* Maryknoll, NY: Orbis, 1997.

Bradshaw, Bruce. *Bridging the Gap: Evangelism, Development and Shalom.* Monrovia, CA: MARC, 1993.

Budziszewski, J. *Evangelicals in the Public Square.* Grand Rapids, MI: Baker, 2006.

Carter, Matt, and Darrin Patrick. *For the City: Proclaiming and Living Out the Gospel.* Grand Rapids, MI: Zondervan, 2011.

Chambers, Robert. *Rural Development: Putting the Last First.* London: Longman, 1983.

———. *Whose Reality Counts? Putting the First Last.* London: Intermediate Technology, 1997.

Chapman, John. *Know and Tell the Gospel.* 2nd ed. Sydney: Matthias Media, 1998.

Chester, Tim. *Awakening to a World of Need: The Recovery of Evangelical Social Concern.* Nottingham, UK: Inter-Varsity, 1993.

———. "Eschatology and Mission: The Kingdom of God Is at Hand." In *What Are We Waiting For? Christian Hope and Contemporary Culture.* Edited by Stephen Holmes and Russell Rook. Carlisle, UK: Paternoster, 2008. See pp. 87–97.

———. ed. *Justice, Mercy and Humility: Integral Mission and the Poor*. Carlisle, UK: Paternoster, 2002.

———. *A Meal with Jesus: Discovering Grace, Community, and Mission around the Table*. Wheaton, IL: Crossway, 2011.

———. *Mission and the Coming of God: Eschatology, the Trinity and Mission in the Theology of Jürgen Moltmann and Contemporary Evangelicalism*. Paternoster Theological Monographs. Carlisle, UK: Paternoster, 2006.

———. *Unreached? Growing Churches in Working-Class and Deprived Areas*. Nottingham, UK: Inter-Varsity, 2012.

DeYoung, Kevin, and Greg Gilbert. *What Is the Mission of the Church? Making Sense of Social Justice, Shalom, and the Great Commission*. Wheaton, IL: Crossway, 2011.

Draycott, Andy, and Jonathan Rowe, eds. *Living Witness: Explorations in Missional Ethics*. Nottingham, UK: Apollos, 2012.

Evangelism and Social Responsibility: An Evangelical Commitment, Lausanne Occasional Paper 21, 1982, http://www.lausanne.org/en/documents/lops /79-lop-21.html.

Fikkert, Brian, and Steve Corbett. *When Helping Hurts: Alleviating Poverty without Hurting the Poor . . . and Yourself*. Chicago: Moody, 2009.

Forrester, Duncan B. *On Human Worth: A Christian Vindication of Equality*. London: SCM, 2001.

Gordon, Graham. *What If I Got Involved? Taking a Stand against Social Injustice*. Carlisle, UK: Paternoster, 2003.

Grant, Jamie A., and Dewi A. Hughes. *Transforming the World? The Gospel and Social Responsibility*. Nottingham, UK: Apollos, 2009.

Greene, Mark. *Thank God It's Monday: Ministry in the Workplace*. 2nd ed. London: Scripture Union, 1997.

Grigg, Viv. *Companion to the Poor*. Sydney: Albatross, 1984.

Gutiérrez, Gustavo. *A Theology of Liberation*. London: SCM, 1974.

Hall, Douglas John. *The End of Christendom and the Future of Christianity*. Harrisburg, PA: Trinity Press, 1995.

Hathaway, Brian. *Beyond Renewal: The Kingdom of God*. Milton Keynes, UK: Word, 1999.

Hatmaker, Brandon. *Barefoot Church: Serving the Least in a Consumer Culture*. Grand Rapids, MI: Zondervan, 2011.

Haugen, Gary. *Good News about Injustice*. Nottingham, UK: Inter-Varsity, 1999.

Hope, Anne, and Sally Timmel. *Training for Transformation: A Handbook for Community Workers, Books I, II and III*. London: Intermediate Technology, 1984.

Horton, Michael. *The Gospel-Driven Life: Being Good News People in a Bad News World*. Grand Rapids, MI: Baker, 2009.

Hudson, Neil. *Imagine Church: Releasing Whole-Life Disciples*. Nottingham, UK: Inter-Varsity, 2012.

Hughes, Dewi A. In collaboration with Matthew Bennett. *God of the Poor*. Carlisle, UK: OM, 1998.

Hughes, Dewi A. *Power and Poverty: Divine and Human Rule in a World of Need*. Nottingham, UK: Inter-Varsity, 2008.

Joslin, Roy. *Urban Harvest*. Darlington, UK: Evangelical Press, 1982.

Keller, Timothy J. *Generous Justice: How God's Grace Makes Us Just*. New York: Dutton, 2010.

———. *Ministries of Mercy: The Call of the Jericho Road*. Phillipsburg, NJ: P&R, 1997.

Kirk, Andrew. *A New World Coming*. London: Marshalls, 1983.

Korten, David C. *Getting to the 21st Century: Voluntary Action and the Global Agenda*. Sterling, VA: Kumarian Press, 1990.

Lupton, Robert D. *Toxic Charity: How Churches and Charities Hurt Those They Help (And How to Reverse It)*. New York: HarperOne, 2011.

Maggay, Melba. *Transforming Society*. Oxford, UK: Regnum, 1994.

Marshall, Paul. *Thine Is the Kingdom*. London: Marshall, Morgan & Scott, 1984.

Maxwell, Simon. *The Meaning and Measurement of Poverty*. ODI Poverty Briefing. London, 1999.

———. *What Can We Do with a Rights-Based Approach to Development?* ODI Briefing Paper. London, 1999.

McCloughry, Roy. *The Eye of the Needle*. Nottingham, UK: Inter-Varsity, 1990.

Mott, Stephen Charles. *Biblical Ethics and Social Change*. Oxford, UK: Oxford University Press, 1982.

———. *A Christian Perspective on Political Thought*. Oxford, UK: Oxford University Press, 1993.

Mouw, Richard. *Political Evangelism*. Grand Rapids, MI: Eerdmans, 1973.

———. *Politics and the Biblical Drama*. Grand Rapids, MI: Baker, 1976.

Myers, Bryant L. *Walking with the Poor: Principles and Practices of Transformational Development*. Maryknoll, NY: Orbis, 1999.

Newbigin, Lesslie. *Foolishness to the Greeks: The Gospel and Western Culture*. Grand Rapids, MI: Eerdmans, 1986.

————. *The Gospel in a Pluralistic Society.* London: SPCK, 1989.

Nicholls, Bruce, ed. *In Word and Deed.* Carlisle, UK: Paternoster, 1985.

O'Donovan, Oliver. *The Desire of Nations: Rediscovering the Roots of Political Theology.* Cambridge, UK: Cambridge University Press, 1996.

————. *Resurrection and Moral Order: An Outline for Evangelical Ethics.* Nottingham, UK: Inter-Varsity, 1986.

Padilla, C. René. *Mission between the Times.* Grand Rapids, MI: Eerdmans, 1985.

Peterson, Jim. *Living Proof: Sharing the Gospel Naturally.* Colorado Springs, CO: NavPress, 1989.

Platt, David. *Radical: Taking Back Your Faith from the American Dream.* Colorado Springs, CO: Multnomah, 2010.

Pretty, Jules N., Irene Guijt, John Thompson, and Ian Scoones. *Participatory Learning and Action: A Trainer's Guide.* London: International Institute for Environment and Development, 1995.

Samuel, Vinay, and Chris Sugden, eds. *The Church in Response to Human Need.* Oxford, UK: Regnum, 1987.

————. eds. *Evangelism and the Poor.* Oxford, UK: Regnum, 1983.

Sider, Ronald, ed. *Evangelicals and Development.* Carlisle, UK: Paternoster, 1981.

————. *Evangelism and Social Action.* London: Hodder & Stoughton, 1993.

————. ed. *Lifestyle in the Eighties.* Carlisle, UK: Paternoster, 1982.

————. *Rich Christians in an Age of Hunger.* London: Hodder & Stoughton, 1977.

Sine, Tom. *Mustard Seed vs. McWorld.* Oxford, UK: Monarch, 1999.

Sire, James W. *Discipleship of the Mind.* Nottingham, UK: Inter-Varsity, 1990.

Smith, David. *Mission after Christendom.* London: Darton, Longman & Todd, 2003.

————. *Seeking a City with Foundations: Theology for an Urban World.* Nottingham, UK: Inter-Varsity, 2011.

————. *Transforming the World? The Social Impact of British Evangelicalism.* Carlisle, UK: Paternoster, 1998.

Starkey, Mike. *Born to Shop.* Oxford, UK: Monarch, 1989.

Stott, John. *Christian Mission in the Modern World.* Eastborne, UK: Kingsway, 1975, 1986.

————. *Issues Facing Christians Today.* London: Marshall, Morgan & Scott, 1984.

————., ed. *Making Christ Known: Historic Mission Documents from the Lausanne Movement 1974–1989.* Carlisle, UK: Paternoster, 1996.

Sugden, Chris. *Radical Discipleship*. London: Marshall, Morgan & Scott, 1981.

Taylor, John V. *Enough Is Enough*. London: SCM, 1975.

Thacker, Justin, and Marijke Hoek, eds. *Micah's Challenge: The Church's Responsibility to the Global Poor*. Carlisle, UK: Paternoster, 2008.

Timmis, Steve, and Tim Chester. *The Gospel-Centred Church*. London: Good Book Company, 2002.

Tinker, Melvin. *Evangelical Concerns*. Fearn, Ross-shire, UK: Mentor, 2001.

Volf, Miroslav. *Exclusion and Embrace: A Theological Reflection on Identity, Otherness, and Reconciliation*. Nashville, TN: Abingdon, 1996.

Wallis, Jim. *The Soul of Politics*. New York: Fount, 1994.

Wolffe, John. *Evangelical Faith and Public Zeal: Evangelicals and Society in Britain 1780–1980*. London: SPCK, 1995.

Wolters, Albert. *Creation Regained*. Carlisle, UK: Paternoster, 1985.

Wright, Christopher J. H. *Living as the People of God: The Relevance of Old Testament Ethics*. Nottingham, UK: Inter-Varsity, 1983.

Wright, N. T. *Jesus and the Victory of God*. London: SPCK, 1996.

———. *The New Testament and the People of God*. London: SPCK, 1992.

Wright, Tom. *The Original Jesus: The Life and Vision of a Revolutionary*. Grand Rapids, MI: Eerdmans, 1997.

General Index

Scripture Index

WEST Porterbrook

Gospel-centred training for the missional Church

Porterbrook LEARNING

- training you to serve Jesus, his people and his world.
- a course designed for all Christians to learn how to live gospel-centred lives on mission to their local context
- no prior theological education required
- whole life training with studies in Bible, doctrine, character, church and mission

Porterbrook SEMINARY

- for church leaders and planters to train in the context of ministry
- an affordable and flexible college level course that prepares people for leadership
- also provides training and experience necessary for further study through GDip (for those who hold a degree in any subject)

WEST
Wales Evangelical
School of Theology

- study with WEST for a GDip conversion degree leading on to the MA in Contemporary Church Leadership and PhD studies
- study campuses include Bridgend in Wales and Sheffield in England from 2014

www.porterbrooknetwork.org

Learn about Church and Community from Tim Chester

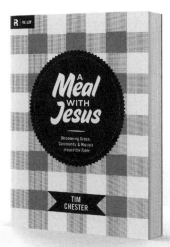

Discovering grace, community, and mission around the table

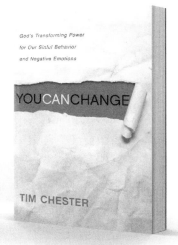

Hope for a change

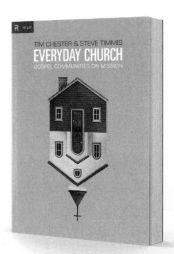

Being the church throughout the week

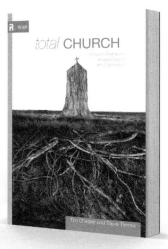

Making church central to life